THE MAKING
OF EFFECTIVE
ADVERTISING

THE MAKING OF EFFECTIVE ADVERTISING

CHARLES H. PATTI
Sonoma State University

SANDRA E. MORIARTY
University of Colorado-Boulder

PRENTICE HALL, Englewood Cliffs, New Jersey 07632

Library of Congress Cataloging-in-Publication Data

PATTI, CHARLES H.
   The making of effective advertising / by Charles H. Patti and
  Sandra E. Moriarty.
      p.   cm.
   Includes index.
   ISBN 0-13-547290-3
   1. Advertising copy. 2. Advertising. I. Moriarty, Sandra E.
  (Sandra Ernst) II. Title.
  HF5825.P28   1990
  659.1-dc20

Editorial/production supervision: *Alison D. Gnerre*
Cover design: *George Cornell*
Manufacturing buyer: *Peter Havens*

 © 1990 by Prentice-Hall, Inc.
A Division of Simon & Schuster
Englewood Cliffs, New Jersey 07632

Printed in the United States of America

10 9 8 7 6 5 4 3 2 1

ISBN 0-13-547290-3

Prentice-Hall International (UK) Limited, *London*
Prentice-Hall of Australia Pty. Limited, *Sydney*
Prentice-Hall Canada Inc., *Toronto*
Prentice-Hall Hispanoamericana, S.A., *Mexico*
Prentice-Hall of India Private Limited, *New Delhi*
Prentice-Hall of Japan, Inc., *Tokyo*
Simon & Schuster Asia Pte. Ltd., *Singapore*
Editora Prentice-Hall do Brasil, Ltda., *Rio de Janeiro*

Contents

2
ANALYSIS OF THE AGENCY STATEMENTS   25

3
IN THEIR OWN WORDS   37

Preface

What is effective advertising? Advertising that gets results? Advertising that gets talked about? Advertising that you like? Effectiveness in advertising is difficult to define. We all know what we like, but advertising is more than a popularity contest. Ultimately, advertising is created to help someone sell something—a product, a service, an idea, or a concept. Eventually, it is judged on its ability to generate the action desired by the advertiser. Sometimes the desired response is a visit to a retail location. Sometimes it is change in attitude. Sometimes it is acceptance of new information. And, sometimes, it is purchase. Because advertising has become such an important business tool, there is greater interest in learning how it works. *The Making of Effective Advertising* explores one aspect of how advertising works—how many of the leading advertising agencies create advertising. Because most of the advertising we see and hear is produced by advertising agencies, we asked them how they work—how they formulate and produce advertising.

TO THE STUDENT OF ADVERTISING

We assembled this book for anyone interested in knowing more about creating advertising. Other works explain the advertising contributions of the well-known figures of advertising, from Volney Palmer to David Ogilvy. We wrote this book with two purposes in mind: first, to pull together many of the various approaches to advertising creativity; and second, to allow many of the creators of advertising to share their thoughts on how they go about their work.

There are many ways to study advertising. If you want to work in the creative areas of advertising, there is no substitute for practice—conceptualizing, writing, and designing. After years of working in advertising and teaching it to thousands of college students, we believe that an effective supplement to practice is to study the process used by advertising practitioners. We hope you will have a greater appreciation for advertising and a stronger understanding of how it is produced through reading and examining the statements and samples in this book.

ORGANIZATION OF THE BOOK

The Making of Effective Advertising consists of three parts. Part 1, "Approaches to Effective Advertising," raises a number of fundamental questions about the nature of advertising; discusses alternative philosophies and functions of advertising; describes the characteristics of effective advertising; and compares alternative approaches to effective advertising.

Part 2, "Analysis of the Agency Statements," places the statements of the thirty-three advertising agencies included in this book into categories of similarity. Although every advertising agency is unique, there are similarities. For example, some agencies tend to focus on the product, while others stress the needs of the intended audience. Some emphasize the details of the message structure, and others take a more generalized market ing approach.

Part 3, "In Their Own Words," shows you precisely how the participating agencies approach their work. Each advertising agency was asked to submit a statement that explains what they feel makes effective advertising and how they create effective advertising. Many of the agencies also submitted samples of their work. The statements were edited only for consistency of format, and the captions for the examples were provided by the agencies. When an agency did not provide a caption we used, "An example of the work of (agency)."

SPECIAL NOTE

The advertising industry is filled with change. Advertisers change agencies and agencies resign accounts. In recent years, there also has been a number of mergers among advertising agencies and advertisers. It is impossible for a book like this to keep up with shifting accounts, mergers, and name changes; therefore, you will notice that some of the information in this book—agency names, locations, and advertisers represented—is no longer current. While account shifts, personnel movement, and mergers can have significant effects within the industry, *The Making of Effective Advertising* is concerned only with how the major U.S. advertising agencies create advertising . . . for past advertisers, current advertisers, or advertisers they hope to work with in the future.

ACKNOWLEDGMENTS

From its beginning, *The Making of Effective Advertising* was dependent on the cooperation of members of the advertising agency business. To collect the material for this book we surveyed the largest 150 advertising agencies in the United States. We are indebted to those agencies that were willing to share their thoughts with us. It is often difficult to explain exactly what you do and how you do it. We congratulate the thirty-three advertising agencies included in this book for their courage in revealing their personalities to us.

In many ways, our students were the inspiration for this book. In our teaching, we are constantly aware of the importance of bringing current thought to the classroom—thought from the world of scholarly research as well as from the day-to-day practice of advertising. Ultimately, the needs of our students encouraged us to collect the material in this book.

Finally, we thank our colleagues who reviewed this book in earlier drafts, gave us many helpful suggestions, and assisted in the collection of some of the materials. We are particularly indebted to Vincent J. Blasko, Arizona State University; Charles F. Frazer, University of Colorado at Boulder; Jerome Jeweler, University of South Carolina; Kathy Judd, University of Denver; Lorraine Harris; and Thomas R. Duncan, University of Colorado at Boulder.

About the Authors

Charles H. Patti, Ph.D. (University of Illinois) is Professor of Marketing, School of Business, Sonoma State University. He formerly served on the faculties of Arizona State University and the University of Denver where he was Chairman of the Department of Marketing and Director of Graduate Studies in Advertising. Professor Patti has also held visiting professorships at the University of Hawaii, the Helsinki School of Economics, and Bocconi University, Milan.

Prior to his career in education, Dr. Patti spent eight years in advertising. He began his advertising career as a copywriter and designer for a book publishing company. Later, after an editorship of a large company magazine, he became director of advertising and public relations for the largest operating division of U.S. Industries, USI-Clearing. Eventually, he became vice president of corporate communications for U.S. Industries, Inc. Dr. Patti continues his involvement in the advertising business through consulting with such companies as American Telephone Advertising, Citicorp, Frontier Airlines, McDonald's, and Mountain Bell.

Dr. Patti's academic research has focused on the major areas of advertising management, and his research has been published in a number of academic and trade journals, including *Journal of Advertising, Journal of Advertising Research, Journal of Marketing*, and *Industrial Marketing Management*. In addition to *The Making of Effective Advertising*, he has coauthored three other books on advertising management, including *Advertising: A Decision-Making Approach*, The Dryden Press, 1988.

Sandra E. Moriarty, Ph.D., is Professor of Advertising, School of Journalism and Mass Communication, University of Colorado. She formerly taught at Michigan State University and the University of Kansas. Her M.S. and Ph.D. are from Kansas State University and B.J. from the University of Missouri.

Prior to teaching, Dr. Moriarty worked in university relations, owned her own advertising and PR agency, worked as copy chief for a retail chain in Seattle, and served as information officer for a government agency in Kansas City.

Dr. Moriarty's research and scholarly writing focuses on visual communication, typography, theories of explanation, message strategy, and creative thinking. Her articles have appeared in *Current Issues and Research in Advertising, Journalism Quarterly, Journal of Applied Psychology, Journal of Creative Behavior, Journal of Visual-Verbal Languaging, Journal of Visible Language*, and *PR Quarterly*.

In addition to *The Making of Effective Advertising*, she has authored or coauthored five other books: *Advertising: Principles and Practices, Creative Advertising: Theory and Practice, How to Create and Deliver Winning Advertising Presentations, The ABCs of Typography*, and *The Creative Package*.

THE MAKING OF EFFECTIVE ADVERTISING

1
APPROACHES TO EFFECTIVE ADVERTISING

While the business of advertising uses businesslike procedures and strategies, with much effort spent on research, analysis, planning, and objectives setting, the creation of advertising is seldom as efficient as business. Ideas come, in many cases, independent of the highly researched and carefully phrased strategy statements, and sometimes they don't emerge, no matter how much effort has gone into the development of the strategy or plan.

ADVERTISING: THE GOOD, THE BEST, AND THE GREAT

The primary measure of efficiency in business is the ability to determine if your work is effective, and that's where advertising seems to be most unbusinesslike—there is no easy way to determine if the advertising is good, successful, or effective. What does "good" mean in advertising—intriguing, intrusive, indelible, or effective in meeting objectives such as communicating an idea, touching an emotion, or eliciting a response from the consumer?

Lou Redmond, who was a highly respected copywriter at Ogilvy and Mather, explained in the agency's house magazine: "One of the things that makes the practice of advertising difficult is the chaos of opinion. There is no agreement on what is a good ad."[1]

Measures of Effectiveness

Sales. Sales figures, the bottom line of business, are affected by many factors, only one of which is advertising. Because of the importance of other factors such as distribution, pricing, packaging, and product development, it is seldom possible to conclude that a product failed or succeeded because of its advertising program. There are occasional exceptions, of course, like direct response and retail, but for most products and services it is hard to prove that the bottom line is affected by the advertising.

Objectives.   Advertising experts argue that the evaluation should be on the basis of the intended communication effects or objectives. The only problem is that, as William Swinyard and Charles Patti explain in a *Journal of Advertising* article on copytesting, "Typically, little attention is paid to what 'best' means, and even to the basic objective of an advertising campaign." This problem was pointed out in a study by Steuart Britt. He found that only 1 percent of 135 "successful" advertising campaigns stated an objective in quantifiable terms. He also found that 24 percent of the campaign results were measured in no other terms than sales.[2]

Awards.   There are award programs within the industry that purport to recognize the "best" advertising. However, these are often disparaged by professionals as "beauty shows" where the awards go to the most aesthetically pleasing work rather than the most effective. There are even standing jokes about "the curse of the Clio," which refers to winning the highly coveted Clio award (advertising's version of the Academy Award) only to have the agency lose the account. The explanation is that, while the advertising was intriguing, it presumably did not sell the merchandise. Some award programs include market information in the judging but, since most industry data is proprietary and it is difficult to know what the impact of the advertising actually is on the bottom line, it is hard to evaluate even on that dimension.

STANDARDS AND EVALUATION

So what makes effective advertising? Or rather, what makes advertising effective? Or good, great, or successful? These questions all ask for some kind of evaluation. Unfortunately, there are no commonly agreed upon standards by which professionals in advertising evaluate good, great, successful, or effective advertising.

Rules and Principles

We have been investigating this question of effectiveness since the early 1980s by reading the work of advertising professionals or practitioners and scholars in advertising and by asking advertising agency professionals how they approach creating great advertising. Many of the leaders have developed principles and rules—some of which are generally agreed upon while others are controversial. Some professionals operate with a carefully defined "house" or agency philosophy; others use philosophies that remain unstated. These *agency philosophies* define the methods used to create advertising and give a distinctive style to the agency's work. Yet there are many professionals who believe that rules and philosophies get in the way of creating great advertising.

David Ogilvy has spent some fifty years studying the advertising process and analyzing research findings about what works and what doesn't. Known for his lists of rules, he observes, "I never cease to be struck by the consistency of consumer reactions to different kinds of headlines, illustrations, layouts and copy—year after year, country after country."[3] Ogilvy's rules are specific and practical and include such suggestions as:

Five times as many people read the headlines as read the body copy.

The headlines that work best are those that promise the reader a benefit.

Headlines that contain *news* are sure-fire.

Headlines with more than 10 words get less readership than short headlines.

Celebrity commercials score above average in recall but below average in selling.

Write body copy in the form of a *story*, but don't write *essays*.

Always try to include the *price* of your products.

Long copy sells more than short.

Many of Ogilvy's rules are included in his books, *Confessions of an Advertising Man* and *Ogilvy on Advertising*.[4]

Sid Bernstein, an astute observer of the field in his long-running column in *Advertising Age*, commented that "David Ogilvy demonstrated once again his proclivity for laying down authoritative, definite, uncompromising rules for the writing of advertising. He has, in the course of his career in advertising, probably enunciated more rules for copywriters than any other three authorities you can name."[5]

Another professional who rivals Ogilvy in rule making is John Caples. Caples, who wrote the legendary direct mail ad, "They Laughed When I Sat Down At the Piano," offered his own set of rules in *How to Make Your Advertising Make Money* and *Tested Advertising Methods*.[6] Another legend, Leo Burnett, who also founded a major agency that bears his name, said, "The work of advertising people is inexact, because any creative process is inexact, and the advertising business, however much it is surrounded with facts and figures is essentially a creative process."[7]

This rule making was the subject of a column by George Lois, an irreverent skeptic who at the time was also chairman of the board and creative director of LOIS/GGK. In his column he criticized those people who claim ownership of practices such as positioning and using the product's name in the concept. After reprimanding the originators of these new-found truths, he concluded by saying, "The *full* truth about great advertising is that it derives from *no* rules."[8]

The fact that there is little agreement about something so basic as rules for the business of advertising indicates the difficulty of arriving at any agreement on what is effective, or great, in advertising.

PHILOSOPHIES

The leaders in the field have tried for decades to explain how they create advertising and to express their visions of what makes advertising great. A review of their writings indicates there are a variety of approaches to effectiveness in advertising. A common factor is that each developed a unique approach to advertising and built their agency's reputation on this individual philosophy.

Individual Approaches

The Product's Inherent Drama.   For example, to Burnett effective advertising uncovered the "inherent drama" in a product. The Burnett agency dramatized the product's personality by using mythical characters and strong visual images that expressed the qualities of a product. His agency is responsible for the creation of these memorable characters: Tony the Tiger, Charlie the Tuna, the Jolly Green Giant, and the Marlboro man.[9]

Brand Image.   Ogilvy, too, focused on the product, but he felt effective advertising made a contribution to the long-term development of a product or brand image rather than providing impact for an immediate sale.[10] Ogilvy explains, "It is almost always the total personality of a brand rather than any trivial product difference which decides its ultimate position in the market."[11] The Hathaway man (a symbol for Hathaway shirts), with his eyepatch and aura of mystery, is an example of a brand image created by Ogilvy.

Selling Proposition.   Fairfax Cone, founder of Foote, Cone & Belding, said that good advertising must immediately make clear what the basic selling proposition is, and that this proposition must be important and presented in personal terms.[12] Under his direction, FC&B created such classic ad campaigns as "You'll wonder where the yellow went" for Pepsodent and "When you care enough to send the very best" for Hallmark.

USP.   Rosser Reeves, chairman of the Ted Bates agency, created advertising that effectively established a "unique selling proposition," a proposition that was both important to the consumer and that set the product apart from the competition. Reeves's contribution to the field, explained in his book *The Reality of Advertising*, was his emphasis on the logic behind the sales message.[13] Examples of this hard-hitting, USP-based advertising approach include "Cleans your breath while it cleans your teeth" for Colgate and "Strengthens bodies in 12 ways" for Wonder Bread.

Artistry.   To Bill Bernbach, founder of Doyle Dane Bernbach, effectiveness was found in artistry. Bernbach never stated an agency philosophy but focused his efforts, and those of his staff, on originality. Effective advertising, he believed, was original, dramatic, and startled people into awareness. He believed in great ideas beautifully executed.[14] In addition to originality, Bernbach's approach was one of the first to address the affective, or emotional, side of the advertising message. Examples of his classic campaigns include "Think Small" for the introduction of the Volkswagen Beetle to the United States and the Avis "We Try Harder" campaign.

Emotion.   Like Bernbach, Hal Riney believes in the power of emotion in advertising. Riney heads his own San Francisco agency, winning awards with his unique approach to advertising. The Bartles & James and Henry Weinhard commercials are vintage Riney, with their unusual but believable characters, wry humor, and subtle style. Riney's ads appeal more to the emotions than to the intellect and rarely do they state any specific, product-related reasons for buying the products.[15]

Consumer Problems.   Tom Dillon, president of BBDO, wrote in a *Journal of Advertising* article that advertising is a form of purposeful communication and its purpose is to affect a human decision.[16] This represents one of the first statements of a consumer-oriented approach. He concluded that "when it does not affect a human decision, it has failed in its function." More specifically, Dillon and BBDO believe that advertising is effective when it answers a human problem. The BBDO approach to advertising was built on this concept of "problem detection." For example, when doing research for a dog food, BBDO found that people weren't concerned as much with nutrition as they were with such problems as "smells bad," "costs too much," and "doesn't come in different sizes for different dogs." The BBDO approach is to focus on these problems, rather than on product features.

Summary of Philosophies

What basic approaches can we identify in this brief review of the masters and their philosophies of advertising? The first approach is to focus on the product. Burnett dramatizes the product's personality and Ogilvy focuses on the long-term brand image. Another approach is to begin with the sales logic. The approach of both Reeves and Cone focuses on the logic behind the sales proposition. Bernbach and Riney are concerned with the arresting message and its impact on the emotions and feelings of the audience. This concern for the prospect is another major approach. Dillon considers consumer problems and decision-making processes. These general approaches—product, sales logic, message, and prospect—are central categories in the classification of approaches to effective advertising (see Figure 1).

Figure 1:   Categories of Philosophies

	Focus
Product	Burnett's "Inherent Drama" Ogilvy's "Brand Image"
Sales Logic	Cone's "Selling Proposition" Reeves's "USP"
Message	Bernbach's "Artistry"
Prospect	Bernbach's and Riney's "Emotions" Dillon's "Problem Detection"

ADVERTISING EFFECTS

In the continuing search for a description of advertising effectiveness, one might also look at the meaning of the word "effective," which can be defined as productive (as in having an intended effect), functional, and impressive or striking. Effective advertising is advertising that works, and by that we mean *advertising that produces a desired effect or results*. But what kind of results or effects?

Measurable Criteria

There is a tendency to want to evaluate advertising in terms of impact on sales. This is criticized by many in marketing and advertising because advertising is only one element in the marketing mix and its impact on the sales level is difficult to isolate. There are others, however, who feel that the most legitimate evaluation of advertising is, in fact, sales. Simon Broadbent, research director at Leo Burnett's London office, is a primary example. He observed in *Advertising Works2*, the volume of case histories from the 1982 IPA awards, that, "advertising earns its keep when without it, or with less of it, the firm would be worse off, selling less of its product and making less profit."[17]

The London-based Institute of Practitioners of Advertising (IPA) has been giving advertising effectiveness awards since 1980 to advertising that can be proven to work against measurable criteria. Broadbent, who was instrumental in starting the awards program, said that many entries in the early years simply didn't qualify because the measurement was sloppy: "The most common claim made was 'We did this, sales or consumer measures did that'." He further explained, "Such an association does not prove advertising had an effect (though it may well have)."[18]

IPA also found that in the early years there was very little overlap between the effectiveness winners and the winners of other industry award programs that focused on creativity. That seems to be changing and there are now Cannes awards and Designers' and Art Directors' awards being given to ads that have also won effectiveness awards. Broadbent observed,

"The frequent contrast between creativity and effectiveness obscures the fact that ads can just as easily be both creative and effective or neither."[19]

Effects Models

In addition to this debate about sales impact and the previously discussed philosophies, one might also look at the "hierarchy of effects" models discussed in personal sales and consumer behavior textbooks. These hierarchy of effects theories propose different ways of analyzing the impact of persuasive messages on their audience.

The classic AIDA formula developed in the 1890s by St. Elmo Lewis, for example, identifies *attention, interest, desire,* and *action.*[20] The first stage is a perceptual one that begins when the message catches the attention of the consumer. As the consumer responds, first with interest and then with desire, the message begins to have some effect on his or her attitudes. The final step, action, describes some kind of behavioral response such as visiting a store or mailing in a coupon.

A model developed in the 1960s by Robert Lavidge and Gary Steiner, called the "learn-feel-do" model, looks at the three components of *cognitive, affective,* and *conative* effects.[21] cognitive refers to processing and understanding information; affective includes attitudes and emotions; and conative is behavioral. The elaborated model includes this set of effects: the ad gains the attention and interest of the consumer, the consumer processes the information, there is an emotional response, and finally the consumer is motivated to act.

The initial effects literature proposes such a hierarchy, or a series of steps, that consumers proceed through from initial attention to the final action. This "staircase of influence" has been challenged in more recent years, principally with the work of Herbert Krugman, who introduced the concept of low and high involvement from the area of learning theory.[22] Krugman's theory is that in low-involvement learning situations the consumer tries the product and then forms an opinion. Instead of learn-feel-do, the low-involvement model follows the do-feel-learn pattern.

Swinyard and Patti explained that in cases where products are not clearly differentiated and the audience has a low involvement with both the medium and the message, such as snacks and beverages, the brand might be anchored in the mind without any attitude change at all. The traditional hierarchy is more likely to occur when the audience is highly involved with the product, such as cars. It also occurs when the products are clearly differentiated, such as computers. In a discussion of Krugman's theory, Swinyard and Patti concluded that, "The effect of advertising thus seems to depend upon audience involvement. Some advertising will 'work' only by changing attitudes; other advertising will 'work' without affecting attitudes."[23]

Another challenge to the traditional staircase model comes from Michael Ray, who proposed multiple hierarchies, or a "three-order model," based on *learning* (learn-feel-do), *dissonance attribution* (do-feel-learn), and *low involvement* (do-learn-feel).[24] In other words, different consumers in different situations buying different types of products respond in different ways.

Moriarty challenged the linear aspect of all these models and proposed a form that looks at three domains in which advertising effects can occur. Within each domain there is a continuum from no effect to major effect.[25] The three domains and their sub-categories are:

> *perception*
> arousal: awareness, interest, excitement
> retention: recognition, recall
>
> *education*
> learning: register, associate, comprehend, differentiate
>
> *persuasion*
> attitudes: emotional appeals, liking, acceptance
> argument: reasons, correction, agreement, counterargument
> behavior: traffic, inquiry, trial, purchase, repurchase

The three domains of advertising are seen as equally important and interdependent, with different levels of effects occurring in all three simultaneously.

Summary of Effects

All of the effects models are attempting to describe what happens in the interaction between a consumer and a product purchase and what the impact of the advertising message is on that process. Nevertheless, there are still disagreements in the literature. There are categories by which these various effects may be classified, regardless of whether the process is seen as linear or simultaneous (see Figure 2). The various models are concerned with *perceptual* impact in such areas as *attention and interest. Learning* is another subject that recurs throughout the literature and its effects include such areas as comprehension and association. *Persuasion* is a critical factor and that includes the *emotional and attitudinal* effects as well as *logical* and *behavioral* ones.

Figure 2:   Categories of Effects

Classification	Effect
Perception	Attention Interest
Learning	Comprehension Association
Persuasion	Attitudes and Emotions Logic Behavior

FUNCTIONS

Inform

Another way to analyze effectiveness might be to look at the literature on these functions. Long time advertising educator C.H. Sandage, for many years head of the University of Illinois advertising program, has discussed the basic functions of advertising and identified two primary roles: *to inform and to persuade.*[26] James Carey, communication dean at the University of Illinois, stated that the primary function of advertising is *to provide market information.*[27] This information function focuses on the cognitive, or learning, component of the effects models.

Need Satisfaction

Sandage also characterized the function of advertising as "the interpretation of the want-satisfying characteristics of the market."[28] This emphasis on the consumer's wants and needs was reiterated by Kim Rotzoll, now head of the Illinois program: "Consumers will respond to advertising only when it corresponds with some need or important want perceived by the individual."[29] To Sandage and Rotzoll effective advertising links the wants and needs of the consumer with the attributes of the product. For example, an ad by Epson features the quick-change features of its printer that lets the user move from computer paper to letterhead to envelope. The ad addresses a serious problem, or need, faced by people who use computer printers. Analyzing the audience and addressing their interests is an important principle in the persuasion literature, so this function also relates to the persuasion effect.

Intrusiveness

Fred Schlinger, vice president for creative research at Leo Burnett, presented a model for advertising effectiveness in a *Journal of Advertising* article. Schlinger's model identifies three basic functions: *attract attention, communicate a message,* and *affect attitudes toward the brand.*[30] While we have already considered the communication, or informational, function as well as affecting attitudes, the persuasive function, Schlinger's model adds the attention factor, which represents a perceptual dimension.

The concept of intrusiveness means the ad is hard to ignore—the audience is *aware* of having seen it. Getting attention, however, which sounds so basic to advertising, is still debated. Many theorists believe that advertising should get attention for the product, but not for itself. Ogilvy, for example, holds that "a good advertisement is one which sells the product *without drawing attention to itself.*" He explained that the viewer or reader should say, "I never knew that before," rather than, "what a clever ad."[31]

Not everyone agrees. Peter Cornish, senior vice president at N W Ayer, mentions how surprised he is to hear a commercial described as "great" when, in his view, it is not. He explains, "Advertising isn't great just because a client liked it, because it scored well in research, or even because it met its marketing objectives." That may sound like heresy, but Cornish goes on to say, "These are simply descriptions of advertising that did what it was supposed to do."[32]

To Cornish, a great advertisement should do more than accomplish the expected. This moves into the realm of the third definition of effective advertising used earlier, which was described as "impressive" or "striking." In his view, "It must get talked about. It must be so unique that it becomes a topic of conversation, not just at the agency and the client's office, but among members of the sales force, the trade, the competition and the general public." He continues, "It must be so audacious that it gets written about in the newspapers, discussed in supermarkets, worried about in boardrooms or even joked about on talk shows." He explains that "When advertising gets talked about, it multiplies the effect of the media budget. It becomes a part of our culture, like 'Where's the beef?' 'Try it, you'll like it' or 'Reach out and touch someone.'"[33] This debate about the function of the attention factor continues to divide advertising professionals.

Sales Logic

Dunn and Barban, in their advertising textbook, give four functions of advertising: develop familiarity with a brand name, shape motives and desires, build believability, and provide a reason for selecting one brand over another.[34] The persuasive function is supported once again in the functions that focus on affecting attitudes, shaping desires and motives, and building believability identified by Schlinger as well as by Dunn and Barban. Dunn and Barban's "reason for selection" refers to the development of a sales logic or argument for purchase, and that is also an important factor in persuasion.

Predisposition or Intention

Russell Colley, originator of the celebrated DAGMAR formula for determining advertising objectives, says that the function of advertising is to create a predisposition to buy. He expects advertising to "create a state of mind that will increase the probability that the brand will be bought."[35] The function of successful advertising, then, is to create that state of mind or intention to buy or try the product. That seems to be the first step in responding to a persuasive message, the beginning of an attitudinal shift.

Transformation

William D. Wells, head of research at DDB Needham, says that the function of brand advertising is to transform the experience of buying and using a branded product. He explains that the experience of giving a watch from Tiffany's is different than the experience of giving a watch from K-Mart.[36] Buying Levis or Calvin Klein jeans is different than buying any other pair of jeans. The experience is different because of the way the advertising message affects consumer perceptions of the product. The message, in other words, transforms the experience and makes the product more attractive.

Summary of Functions

The primary functions of effective advertising, then, can be summarized as (1) to inform; (2) to persuade by affecting attitudes, shaping motives and desires, building believability, transforming the experience, and creating a predisposition to buy; and (3) to attract attention and build awareness (see Figure 3).

Figure 3: Classifications of Functions

Classification	Function
Information	Inform
Persuasion	Create Need Satisfaction Affect Attitudes Present Sales Logic Establish Intention/Predisposition Transform Experience
Perception	Attract Attention Build Awareness

TESTS

There are testing services that presume to measure advertising effectiveness. We have already discussed the problems in analyzing advertising effectiveness in terms of sales. Specific campaigns may be evaluated against carefully stated objectives. Much advertising, however, is evaluated using commercial testing programs that compare ads on general characteristics such as recognition and recall. The structure of these tests might give us some idea of what the industry is presently using, rightly or wrongly, as indicators of effectiveness.

There are a number of different testing services, but we will just consider three of the most common ones here. For example, the Starch testing service reports how well a print ad was *noted or seen* by its audience, how well the ad was *associated* with the advertiser's product, and how well the ad was *read*. The Gallup and Robinson Service measures an advertisement's intrusiveness in terms of *name registration*, its communication of a *central idea*, and its persuasiveness in terms of the creation of a *favorable buying attitude*. The Burke tests analyze day-after-recall of television commercials to determine viewers' level of *brand name recognition* and their *recall of the various selling points* communicated by the commercial. Burke scores primarily reflect *intrusiveness* (the ability to break through viewers' inattention or indifference), and copywriters know that to get a high Burke score they must create highly intrusive ads.

Summary of Testing

In general, the four areas being measured by these testing services include: (1) intrusiveness, (2) communication, (3) attitude formation, and (4) brand identification (see Figure 4). Intrusiveness means the ad is attention-getting and hard to ignore. Communication involves delivering some kind of message either factual or emotional. Attitude formation usually means the audience has positive feelings about the product after hearing the message and would like to try it. Brand association means the message is linked with the brand to insure that the audience doesn't forget the product while remembering the ad.

Figure 4:   Classifications of Testing

Classification	Testing Focus
Intrusiveness	Starch: noted/seen
Communication	Starch: read most Gallup and Robinson: central idea Burke: selling points
Attitude Formation	Gallup and Robinson: favorable buying attitude
Brand Identification	Starch: associated Burke: brand identification

CHARACTERISTICS OF EFFECTIVE ADVERTISING

While it is still difficult to define effectiveness in advertising, we have identified a number of characteristics discussed in the literature as well as in the industry. In general, effective advertising strategies focus on the *product* and the appropriate brand image as well as on the *message* or the *prospect.* It communicates a message in a way that is *intrusive and arresting.* The *sales logic* should be clear and compelling. Finally, the advertising should *affect consumers* in some way—either by touching their emotions, affecting their attitudes, transforming their experiences, or adding to their information level.

Effective advertising, then, could be summarized as advertising that successfully manipulates the following seven basic elements:

the right information
with the right touch of intrusiveness

and the right sales logic
and the right brand association and image

   to the right audience
      speaking to the right set of wants and needs
      to create the right attitudinal and emotional response

The word "right" is repeated here because there are many ways to approach any advertising problem and it is important to acknowledge this variety of options. This is where strategy comes in.

STRATEGY AND EFFECTIVENESS

The concept of *strategy*, a military term, can be defined as a plan of action for reaching a goal or objective. There are always a number of ways to reach any objective. The question is how to use limited resources to most efficiently reach the goal. Strategy identifies all the various options and determines which of the alternatives is "right" for the individual situation and which combination will most likely accomplish the goal. Strategy also prioritizes the options and decides where emphasis should be placed given the reality of limited resources. That is why it is possible for advertising to be effective strategically and not be great aesthetically.

ISSUES IN ADVERTISING EFFECTIVENESS

While we can summarize the characteristics of effective advertising and develop categories in which to place examples of such advertising, there are still differences of opinion regarding how to approach creating effective advertising.

Likability

There are even some puzzling contradictions. For example, Draper Daniels asked if advertising "must be loved to be effective."[37] William D. Wells turned the question around in a speech to an advertising research association when he asked, "Must an ad be disliked to be effective?"[38] Obviously these two views represent extremes in the approach to advertising effectiveness.

The issue of whether or not the public likes an advertisement, however, is an important one. The proponents of hard-sell package goods advertising frequently say that it is irrelevant whether the consumer likes the advertising as long as he or she remembers and buys the product. That explains the phenomenon of Mr. Whipple and Charmin, the campaign for a major product that many people love to hate—they hate the campaign, not the product. That's an important distinction, because the opposite can also be true. People can like a campaign and not like, or buy, the product.

But the critical issue is whether advertising needs to be liked to be effective. Many advertising objectives focus on the creation of positive feelings about the ad, the people in the ad, and, by association, the product. That's clearly an important aspect of advertising. John O'Toole, the chairman of Foote, Cone & Belding, expressed this concern when he wrote, "I worry even more about the effectiveness of advertising when large portions of a national sample express doubt about its truth and accuracy. Wouldn't advertising work better if consumers liked it better?"[39] There seems to be no agreement on an answer to this question.

Entertainment

A related issue is the value of entertainment in advertising. Many advertising professionals denigrate the entertainment function because they have learned that many clients aren't moved by such considerations. The Ted Bates Agency, with its emphasis on USPs, relies heavily on doctors and other experts in white coats advising the consumer on the reasons why its client's product is the best. Caples, in his many lists of rules, says: Show the product in use, the reward of using the product and its appeal to the reader's self-interest, or announce something newsworthy. All of these are straightforward sales pitches.

But while many experts in advertising who focus closely on the bottom line believe wholeheartedly in such approaches, there are others who believe that advertising has to be entertaining to sell. For one thing, it has to compete in its own environment and on television that means the advertising has to be as entertaining as the programming that surrounds it.

Many professionals are reluctant to admit that they believe in entertaining advertising, and they will qualify its use by tying the entertainment value to a product characteristic. Bernbach, for example, advised creatives to "be provocative. But be sure your provocativeness stems from the product."[40]

But some experts, like Lois, are not afraid to admit that effective advertising can be zany. He explains, "If you have what you consider a fantastic concept, you must drive it to the precipice. If you don't take it to the edge, you've chickened out. But if you want to do *great* advertising, you'll push your thought to the very rim of insanity. To the very edge."[41]

One very successful advertising professional who really isn't an adperson, but rather a satirist/humorist, is Stan Freberg. Since 1956 he has been making fun of advertising and, much of the time, he is using ads for real clients to lampoon the industry. In his campaigns for such companies as Jeno's Pizza, Encyclopaedia Britannica, and Heinz Great American Soups, he satirizes 800 numbers, direct response ads, and anything that sounds like hard sell. And it seems to work. In addition to twenty-one Clios and other broadcasting and film awards, his campaign for Sunsweet Prunes, "Today the Pits, Tomorrow the Wrinkles," is reported to have increased sales by 400 percent.[42]

Freberg entered advertising to correct what he says is its great mistake:

"It just occurred to me in the mid-50s that most of advertising missed the mark with me and I was motivated to go into it as an outraged consumer." He explains, "Why did they have to treat me like a moron who has to have something drummed into my head over and over?" Freberg concludes, "The secret is to make it appear almost like non-advertising. Don't convey the image that the company thinks they are selling pieces of the Holy Grail. After all, it's just a set of books, a prune or whatever.[43]

Freberg was enticed into the advertising business by Howard Gossage, an iconoclastic San Francisco advertising professional, who has been variously characterized as "the adman who hated advertising" and "the Socrates of San Francisco." Gossage was in the advertising business in the 1950s and 1960s. He had a traditional agency and a list of clients, but he worked strictly on his own terms and with an originality and creativity that made his work distinctively nontraditional.

His entertaining approach to advertising is evident in the strategy he recommended to his client, Rainier Ale. Gossage learned that a 79-year-old postal worker was planning to walk from San Francisco to Seattle to protest his forced retirement. He convinced Rainier to sponsor the postal worker's walk. It was ingenious, in part, because the intense media coverage eliminated the need for ads to promote the protest. Gossage also suggested that the beer company sponsor Brahms, Beethoven, and Bach sweatshirts for his favorite classical music station (KSFR-FM). The sweatshirts carried the slogan, "A brewer's idea of culture," and sweatshirt orders eventually exceeded 200,000.[44]

The Eagle Shirt Company, which hadn't advertised in forty years, asked Gossage for an image campaign. The company supplied shirts for private label retailers, and while business was good, the company was concerned that it was not considered a supplier of high quality men's shirts. Gossage designed the "Dear Miss Afflerbach" campaign, which offered a 'free Eagle shirt-kerchief (shirtkin?) (napchief?). This "shirt-kerchief" was a sample of the shirt material, showing the company's quality stitching and its "threadchecked buttonholes." There were 11,342 replies, which set an all-time record for a *New Yorker* ad. The "Dear Miss Afflerbach" campaign, along with its correspondence, was later published in a 200-page book.[45]

Gossage's credo explains why his work is so memorable: "People don't read advertising. They read what interests them. And sometimes it's an ad." His trademark is an indirect style that uses long copy, a frivolous contest, and a reply coupon. The heart of his philosophy, however, is that advertising should involve the audience and that they should be rewarded for attending to the message. The reward may provide entertainment, information, or simply the satisfaction of reducing their curiosity.[46]

Science or Art

This discussion of straightforward sales messages versus entertaining messages reflects the two streams of thought that have been operating in advertising from its earliest days. The first is the *scientific approach*, which uses research, analysis, and planning to arrive at strategically sound decisions. The second is the *artistic approach*, which uses professional judgment and artistic intuition to arrive at aesthetically pleasing programs.

At different times one approach has been emphasized over the other. Malcolm MacDougall, president of SSC&B, points out that in the 1960s there was a creative revolution, "when showmanship was more important than salesmanship." In contrast, he calls the 1970s the years of the marketing revolution, when "what you said was all that mattered" and that was determined by "the dilation of someone's pupil, by the secretion of certain glands, by the pitch of a child's voice. . . ."[47]

Actually, the debate started much earlier than the 1960s. Caples, who was in the business for about fifty years, said that, "the key to success in advertising (maximum sales per dollar) lies in perpetual testing of all variables."[48] Ogilvy, who also is a student of direct response and an admirer of Gallup, has always been interested in what works and what doesn't work and continues to commission research from Gallup and Robinson and the Starch Readership Service.

Research is used in advertising for market analysis as well as copytesting. Marion Harper, CEO first of McCann-Erickson and then Interpublic, which was the first of the mega-merger advertising holding companies, was described in his biography as a "marketing genius" with "keen research instincts." His biographer explains that Harper "had an amazing ability to extract information from printed material rapidly and under the most difficult conditions—and remember it." He could amaze clients with his ability to recite and analyze massive amounts of data and give the clients the impression that he, the president of one of the world's largest agencies, knew as much about the business and had as much insight into its problems as they did.[49]

On the other side are the skeptics who feel they are experts on advertising and that is the business they should know. To them, research and strategy may be necessary *to communicate* with MBAs but contribute very little to the actual creation of advertising. Burnett, for example, had little patience with copytesting. He has been described as viewing "most quantified copytesting results with an equanimity bordering on indifference." He often said, "Cold logic can smother a hot idea" and "Research that can adequately and conclusively pretest the long-term selling effectiveness of ideas has not yet been invented."[50]

Charlie Brower, CEO at BBDO until he retired in 1970, shared similar views with Burnett. "I think research is great at counting heads but lousy at looking inside of them," he observed. He believed that "research can kill good ideas, as well as bad ones." The solution to decision making, he felt, required intuition and experienced judgment.[51]

Shirley Polykoff, a copywriter for Foote, Cone and Belding and author of the famous "Does she or doesn't she" and "Is it true blondes have more fun" campaigns, looks at research and strategy with a great deal of scorn. About research she observed, "Clients have found it necessary to fortify themselves with a whole battery of research tools that masquerade as crystal balls." She deplores this "fail-safe attitude" of contemporary marketers, with its overreliance on research and strategy. She believes this attitude has lead to dull advertising that is nothing more than a creative platform in print.[52]

Polykoff observed, "These strategies, worked over by a cast of thousands, are supposed to lull the copywriter and client into the lovely notion that the art of advertising is not an art but a science. The important thing is to find the right formula. "Right" in the strategy statement is the recipe for success." She concludes, "It seems to me lately that writing good ads is no longer an art but a mathematical formula."[53]

Bernbach, of course, was the father of the artistry approach to advertising and he explained what Polykoff meant about the art of writing good ads. "The most gossamer things like the expression on a woman's face or the heart-touching appeal of her smile or the grace with which she walks, can make a difference between a commercial that works and one that doesn't."[54] As Bernbach said, "The difference is in the fingertips," not in the test results.

The solution to this debate is easy to see but hard to achieve—to integrate the creative idea with the strategy statement. MacDougall calls this "the best of both worlds—smart strategy and brilliant execution working beautifully together."[55]

One creative leader who seems to accomplish this integration of strategy and execution is Phil Dusenberry, executive creative director at BBDO and creator of the lavish, damn-the-cost "lifestyle" advertising that Pepsi pioneered with its "Pepsi Generation" campaign. Ron Cox, vice president of marketing at Wrigley, says, "What Phil has done is marry how you say it to the strategy." He explains, "There's been a resurgence of that approach in the last three years and Phil is one of the premier people doing it."[56]

Emotion or Straightforward Approach

We have discussed the straightforward approach, with its strong product claims, demonstrations, and experts in white coats; however, there is another school that feels effective advertising must be affective, or touch emotions, in order to move people. The debate continues between those who believe in appealing to people's intellect and others who believe in appealing to the heart.

N W Ayer, with its "human contact" philosophy, is a leader in this genre. Its award-winning "Reach out and touch someone" campaign for the Bell System is a classic example of the approach, as is the Army's "Be all you can be" campaign. The "human contact" philosophy is built on the little things in life that make warm connections between people. Lou Hagopian, Ayer CEO, says that, "The very same things that have been moving your mind and your heart and influencing your feelings all your life are the things that make the great ads." N W Ayer uses points of contact, rather than hard sell, to reach audiences. Hagopian says, "It's far more efficient to touch people with warmth and an understanding of their concerns than to impose your message on them and hope that your name sticks."[57]

Another modern-day believer in the power of emotion is Riney, who rarely states reasons for buying any of the products he advertises. Instead he "appeals more to the emotion than to the intellect." He explains why. "We're asking advertising to depend too much on the rational, and much less, or not at all, on the *effective* element of our business, which is *emotion*." Riney believes in getting into the minds of people and understanding what really moves them. To do that you have to move beyond what people say and how they respond to testing. According to Riney, "The rational element is often merely what people use to justify emotional decisions. Knowing when and how to use emotion is the most important part of an advertising person's job."[58]

People or Product

This discussion of emotion is very similar to another debate that continues concerning where the focus of the advertising should be. In earlier days, the focus was almost exclusively on the product—its features and attributes, claims about its performance, and demonstrations of its use. The revolution in marketing that led to the development of the *marketing concept* (with its emphasis on consumer needs, wants, and behavior) was mirrored in advertising, where the emphasis shifted from features to benefits. The ads now focused on what the product could do for the consumer. Both schools continue to be used in contemporary advertising.

"User image" advertising is used by Dusenberry to integrate the strategy with the execution. "Rather than sanctify the product, we exalt the people who use it," Dusenberry explains. And with his focus on people comes a skillful use of advertising's emotional element. The "We bring good things to life" campaign for General Electric is an example of Dusenberry's heart-tugging spots, of everyday people enjoying the big and little moments of life. "I gotta believe," he says, "that *people*, real people, attractive people, photographed with honesty and affection and fun, are pure magic for churning up the emotional response."[59]

O'Toole, a thoughtful commentator on the role of advertising, also believes that the secret to effective advertising is in touching the individual, and that it helps to communicate with *a person* rather than with *people*. He says, "When the chord is struck in one, the vibrations reverberate in millions."[60]

What or How

All of these issues—the debates over science or art, strategy or intuition, head or heart—are reviewed in the debate of what you say versus how you say it. Throughout the literature, there are writers supporting both sides. Caples, for example, states with conviction that "what you say is more important than how you say it."[61]

The debate was probably best summarized in an *Advertising Age* article by Gerry Scorse, vice president and creative supervisor at N W Ayer, that analyzed "Ogilvy versus Bernbach." Scorse pointed out that both agree on the primacy of the product, but beyond that they fundamentally disagree. Ogilvy's "number one ingredient in his recipe for successful advertising" is: "What you say is more important than how you say it." Bernbach, on the other hand, felt that *what* you say is just the starting point. He said, "Finding out what you say is the beginning of the communication process. How you say it makes people look and listen and believe."[62]

APPROACHES TO ADVERTISING

The purpose of this discussion is to look at approaches to advertising, and to do that we need to know how to recognize and categorize an approach. When you ask professionals how they approach creating an advertisement, they are likely to respond that they start with strategy or research, or maybe they will say that they search for the unexpected idea or for a dramatic creative concept. Such comments suggest that they see the creation of advertising as a process and different professionals begin at different points in the process. Furthermore, they are likely to focus more of their efforts on different aspects of the process.

This is one way, then, to analyze "approach"—by looking at the *beginning step* in the process approach. In other words, it may be possible to identify an approach by looking at the point where the professional begins work. Another way to analyze approach is to look at some *guiding philosophy*. The Burnett approach, for example, focuses on the inherent drama of a product, while the Ogilvy approach focuses on creating an enduring brand image.

While all advertising leaders try to create "effective" advertising, each may have a unique approach to how he or she creates advertising. Five basic categories of approaches can be identified (see Table 1).

The Survey

Since the early 1980s we have been asking *Advertising Age's* largest 150 agencies to tell us how they approach creating effective advertising and to send copies of the work they have created that demonstrate their various approaches. Their work in response to the 1988 survey is presented for the first time in this published volume.

Additional Agency Approaches.   Each agengy responded with a statement describing its approach. There were some general trends that made it possible to group these responses into the broad categories outlined in Table 1. Most of the agency statements could be categorized using this list, but a number of them approach advertising from different avenues.

For example, some of the statements describe a broad approach that

TABLE 1:   Agency Approaches to Effective Advertising

Product

The Product Approach. Focuses on product features and performance
The Brand Approach. Focuses on brand images and the associations that transform the experience of using the brand

Prospect

The Consumer Approach. Focuses on the wants and needs of the audience and their buying behavior and decision making patterns

Message

The Informative Approach. Focuses on a straightforward presentation of information
The Inventive Approach. Focuses on the originality of the message to create intrusiveness and attention-getting effects

Persuasion

The Sales Logic Approach. Focuses on the logic of the sales message and selling premises such as USPs, benefits, promises, and reasons why
The Affective Approach. Focuses on affecting audience attitudes and emotions, shaping their motives and desires, and building believability

Strategy

The Marketing Approach. Focuses on developing a strategy based on a foundation of research, the identification of problems and opportunities,and the development of objectives to solve the problems
The Integrated Approach. Focuses on the appropriate linkage of elements of the strategy with the message execution

covers many, if not most, of the categories of approaches in Table 1. There seems to be more of this kind of response than there is of a carefully developed philosophy or process approach. We use the phrase *multifocused*, or "all inclusive," to describe the work of these agencies.

This current collection of agency statements indicates a continuing emphasis on various strategy-related activities. A number of them emphasize the need for research as a foundation for all other efforts. Another set of responses outlines the use of a plan, and we call that technique *the disciplined approach.*

Several of the agencies describe how they organize their staff to create effective advertising, and we refer to their method as *the organizational approach.*

One other interesting observation that comes from reviewing the agencies' statements and comparing them against our list of standard approaches is that none of these statements center on an affective approach. In other words, none of these agencies base their philosophy of effective advertising on "touching people" and creating messages that alter peoples' emotions and feelings. Two agencies, however, do refer to affective advertising as important, if not the most central aspect, of their philosophy.

Another technique that received little emphasis in the agency statements is the approach that focuses on product features and performance claims. Some statements refer to the importance of product performance, but only one tries to build a philosophy on that approach. The revised list of approaches, then, includes the 12 categories shown in Table 2.

TABLE 2

Product
  1. The Product Approach
  2. The Brand Approach

Prospect
  3. The Consumer Approach

Message
  4. The Informative Approach
  5. The Inventive Approach

Persuasion
  6. The Sales Logic Approach
  7. The Affective Approach

Strategy
  8. The Marketing Approach
  9. The Disciplined Approach
10. The Integrated Approach

Organization
11. The Organizational Approach

Varied
12. The Multifocused Approach

The complete agency statements may cover elements from a number of these approaches, but we are looking at streams of thought and overall emphasis. For example, an agency report may begin by saying that research is important. However, because the agency believes this is obvious, the report then focuses on the importance of the development of original ideas. If an agency's work is categorized as following the *inventive approach*, it doesn't mean that its team isn't disciplined or doesn't produce creative strategy statements. The labeling of a general approach doesn't limit an agency's approach; it is just an attempt to focus it within an overall field of work.

A Multilayered, Multidimensional Model

What also is apparent from reading the agency statements and looking at their work is that developing an approach for creating effective advertising is a very complex task. Some agencies are able to be tightly focused on an individual philosophy; others aren't and don't want to. What it also suggests is that the answer to the question of how to approach doing effective advertising is multilayered and multidimensinal (see Figure 5).

The *product*, with its subcategories, and the *prospect* are both on the foundation level. The *message* that is addressed to the prospect about the product is another category. The various elements of *strategy* and the identification of the appropriate *persuasive* approach is a separate level. Finally, there is the level made up of the *organization* of the people who do the

Figure 5: Advertising Focus

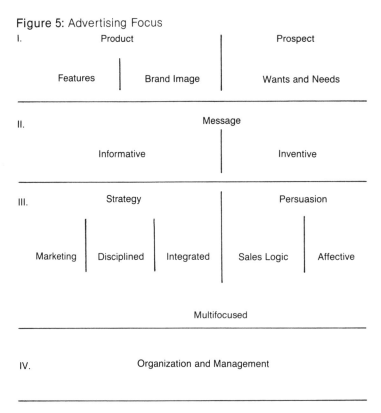

work. There is nothing hierarchical about what we are calling levels—it is just a way of separating the four general categories of approaches. This could be depicted in a complex form as a four-dimensional model, or it could be expressed in a more simplified form as four layers or four concentric circles or four pieces of a pie. For simplicity's sake, we have used a four-level model.

2
ANALYSIS OF THE AGENCY STATEMENTS

THE RESPONSES

The following discussion analyzes the agency responses in terms of advertising effectiveness and approaches to creating advertisements. This section categorizes agency statements in terms of how they approach the question of effectiveness. Part 3 includes the complete agency statements plus samples of their work.

The Product

The Product Approach.   Only one of the agencies responded with an approach that focuses clearly on product features or performance claims. Asher/Gould Advertising, a Los Angeles agency, states: "We believe in performance claims" and most of this agency's advertising is built on performance claims such as tastier chicken, more videotapes, and so on. Asher/Gould explains: "We accept the challenge of building our advertising around 'the best possible claim,' even if that claim has been usurped by a competitor. It is our job to find a different and better way to execute the 'high-ground strategy.'"

The Brand Image Approach.   Many more agencies, however, emphasize the brand image approach to effective advertising. This is probably a result of the growth in the number of parity, or undifferentiated, products. In a category where there is little difference among the products, the advertising will very likely turn to image advertising in order to create a "perceived difference."

Grey Advertising, for example, is well known for its long-time emphasis on brand character. Brand character is an added dimension that tells what the brand is, and what makes it recognizable and appealing to consumers. Grey says, "The advertising that helps create that strong Brand Character™, has a look, a sound, a feeling as personal—as identifiable—as those characteristics which distinguish one person from another." Grey sees Brand Character™ as something that endures over the years.

BBDO focuses on brand imagery as a technique to differentiate products that are basically very similar. BBDO explains, "From advertising, people experience *images* of the product and its performance, and *images* of the users—people the advertiser associates with the product." The BBDO philosophy is summarized in this statement: "The key thing we must remember is this: It's all images."

The Prospect

The Consumer Approach.   Advertising that focuses on the audience is concerned with consumer behavior, needs, interests, and attitudes. This is a relatively new orientation in advertising and parallels the development of the "marketing" concept in business, which focuses on developing products based on consumer needs. The consumer-oriented agencies are often found in special-interest promotion categories that target groups such as women, blacks, Hispanics, or youth.

Griffin Bacal, for example, is a New York agency that is a recognized leader in youth marketing. The youth market is considerably different from the generalized adult population, and communicating with them takes a different style, tone, and technique. Griffin Bacal explains: "To reach them and motivate them, Griffin Bacal talks to them in their own language, on their own terms."

Long, Haymes & Carr, a North Carolina agency, is discussed in more detail under "The Integrated Approach," but the emphasis on relevance to the consumer is strong in this agency's statement. The agency begins its planning with some product truth that "offers the most promise to the consumer." It feels that great advertising "is advertising that has been given a consumer relevant interpretation."

The Message

Advertising is the development of a commercial message, so it makes sense that a number of agencies would focus on the message and their role in developing it as central to effective advertising. Basically there are two approaches that are concerned with the message—one focuses on a straightforward informative message; the other focuses on inventive, creative, and original messages that are attention getting and intrusive.

The Informative Approach.   In the informative category is A. Eicoff & Company, a Chicago agency that specializes in new product introductions. The A. Eicoff statement says, "Our task is to not only produce quality work, but produce work that gets results." This agency strives to "create commercials that viewers respond to" and also to strengthen the image of the client.

Asher/Gould agency was introduced earlier under the discussion of product-oriented approaches. This agency also describes itself as "a content agency." The key to this agency's philosophy is this statement: "What you say is more important than how you say it." The statement explains: "We do not regard advertising as an art form. We are paid to move people to do things. To sell." In contrast, or perhaps as a challenge to the inventive approach (highlighted in the following section), Asher/Gould states: "Unless the strategy is correct, the creative work, no matter how clever, brilliant, funny, or touching, will fail."

The Inventive Approach.   The opposite approach to the straightforward, informative approach is to emphasize the creative or inventive dimension. The TBWA agency has an answer for the Asher/Goulds of the industry when it observes: "We believe in proper positioning and the need for advertising to be sales-oriented . . . but we do not belabor these tenets because they are so obvious." The TBWA statement continues: "Perhaps you have noticed, as we have, that the agencies which spend all their time pontificating about the 'givens' (positioning and sales) tend to be the agencies which produce the dullest advertising." TBWA, on the other hand, says, "We believe in the importance of the advertising execution itself . . . that how you say it is often as important as what you say." The agency's statement explains: "The most brilliant copy strategy in the world is worthless if the advertising is invisible. People remember ads, not strategies."

Della Femina, Travisano & Partners, an agency well known for its approach to creative advertising, explains why originality is so important. "Our philosophy is to realize that very few consumers lie awake at night thinking about advertising, and at best, they don't care about it. Realizing this, it is our objective to strike a bargain with them: We will interest or entertain them for a while so that they will listen to our message." Della Femina's emphasis on executional technique produces messages that are interesting and entertaining. It is worth noting that agencies that believe wholeheartedly in straightforward informative advertising would be reluctant to admit to doing "entertaining" advertising. The word "entertaining" is a red flag to some agencies—and their clients.

George Lois, in the statement he wrote for his agency, LOIS/GGK, addresses the controversy between what is said and how it is said by suggesting a combination of the two. He observes, "We believe that great advertising not only conveys what has to be said about a product—it also does it with a sense of theater and style that makes the creative product memorable and effective." He believes in the power of the execution itself: "Great advertising, we believe, in and of itself, is a benefit of the product." In other words, one of the product's most important features may be its advertising. Once again, a statement that would sound like heresy to the "straight information" school of advertising.

An Austin, Texas agency known as GSD&M discusses the problem of turning advertising from an uninvited guest in people's homes to an invited guest. This agency's statement focuses on some of the same characteristics as Della Femina and LOIS/GGK. Two of the three "musts" are in the creative or inventive mode. First they say: "We must intrigue them—captivate them with the way we look, the things we say." Then they say: "We must entertain them—encourage them to laugh, or at least smile. . . ."

Al Paul Lefton, a New York agency, is concerned with three terrible truths: that the prospect isn't sitting around waiting for the ad; that the prospect won't work at it; and that the prospect has no interest in remembering the message. Lefton believes effective advertising comes from creative executions that are:

- arresting—to get our prospect's attention
- clear—to be understood
- distinctive—to be sure our prospect remembers not only what was said, but also who said it.

Persuasion

There are two primary ways to persuade people with advertising messages. One is to touch their minds and the other is to touch their hearts. Advertising, through its history, has swung back and forth between these two approaches. The agencies reviewed in this book are more inclined to use selling premises ("The Sales Logic Approach"), and less likely to emphasize emotions and feelings ("The Affective Approach"). Selling premises include all of the various phrases used to talk about the logic behind the appeal such as benefits, reasons why, and unique selling propositions.

The Affective Approach.   None of the agencies built their primary approach on emotions and feelings. However, the GSD&M agency, discussed earlier under "The Inventive Approach," touched on the affective approach in its statement. GSD&M includes affective responses in its description of the entertainment function of the message. For example, it says: "We must entertain them—encourage them to laugh, or at least smile; to cry, or at least feel empathy."

Altschiller Reitzfeld, a New York agency discussed later under "The Integrated Approach," is also concerned with the affective side of advertising. Altschiller tries to establish an "emotional bond" between product and consumer. The statement explains: "By tone of voice, by language, by empathy, the consumer comes to believe that the product or service being offered 'understands' his needs. . . ."

A similar philosophy is expressed in the statement prepared by the agency LGFE. This agency believes that "good advertising shares one central characteristic—it creates a connection on an emotional level between the consumer and the brand."

There are major agencies not reviewed here who are identified with this approach, so it is probably incorrect to conclude that this approach is rarely used. However, it clearly isn't in vogue with this group of agencies.

The Sales Logic Approach.   Interestingly, the GSD&M statement touches on both aspects of the persuasion model and includes a statement about sales logic as well as feelings. The third characteristic of what the agency describes as successful advertising is reviewed in this statement: "We must persuade them—convince them that what we have to offer is genuinely unique and valuable to them."

Unique and valuable is part of the Unique Selling Proposition, or USP, formula, as described by Rosser Reeves. The USP is both unique to the product and important to the prospect. Weightman Advertising of Philadelphia is one agency that focuses on USPs as an agency approach. Weightman's statement says: "We believe that for every product or service there is a Unique Selling Proposition, and we search until we find it." Recognizing that, in the age of parity products, it may be difficult at times to find a benefit that is truly unique, Weightman modifies the traditional product difference approach to include a preemptive approach. The statement says: "It may not be a real difference, but simply a preemptive presentation of a shared benefit." In other words, the USP approach can be expanded to include sales messages that claim a unique benefit simply by getting there first and beating out the competition.

Probably the simplest and most universal of the selling premises is a benefit statement. Benefits express the product's value in terms of what it will do for the consumer—in other words, what the prospect gets out of the purchase or use of the product. One agency, Liggett*Stashower of Cleveland, responded with a strong benefit approach: "We work to identify the primary benefit of the product or its unique reason-for-being. . . ." While the agency focuses on benefits, its search for a product's unique reason-for-being moves it closer to a USP approach.

Strategy

We have been talking about the logical dimension in persuasion, but sales logic is also a very important part of strategic planning. Even though sales logic is placed under persuasion rather than strategy in this particular outline, remember that decisions about selling premises are central to the overall advertising strategy.

Under the heading of strategy we have included approaches that focus on a variety of different topics. Some emphasize research and analysis of the competitive situation in the marketplace. Others approach advertising by following a clearly defined plan or procedure. Another group tries to identify critical factors in the marketing situation, whether in the categories of product or consumer, and then link them together with the message execution technique through some bond of association or logic.

The Marketing Approach.   The Keller Crescent Agency from Evansville, Indiana, is a strong marketing oriented agency that also focuses on identifying a primary selling idea. Keller Crescent's statement begins: "Advertising's only role is an execution that solves your marketing problems." The statement explains the focus of the agency's efforts: "We don't raise a pencil or a squeaky pen until we've isolated through client input, marketing, research, and judgment the *one* major selling idea appropriate to a brand or an idea." This agency also could have been included in the previous discussion on the sales logic of the message.

Carmichael Lynch of Minneapolis states, "Our mission is to be a creative company." Yet the definition of creative is productive rather than inventive. The statement cites a number of agency characteristics, but its dedication to marketing is most prominent: "We are dedicated to a disciplined process in strategic marketing planning and advertising parts of our business." In a discussion of the marketing communications discipline, the Carmichael Lynch statement reveals: "We will follow a proven methodology . . . a marketing process, taking into account the full marketing mix . . . product, pricing, distribution and promotion. We dedicate ourselves to knowing the marketing communication issues of our clients' businesses as well as they do, spending their money as if it were ours." They conclude the discussion with a statement that defines their view of strategy: "We will avoid 'hip shots' and stress the methodological sifting of alternative strategies and plans."

Levine, Huntley, Schmidt and Beaver, of New York, focuses on marketing research and clearly defined objectives. This agency's statement says: "We create advertising simply by acquiring as much knowledge as we can—about the product, the marketplace, the competition, and, above all, the attitude of the consumer." Levine, Huntley doesn't limit itself to strategic considerations, but it seems clear that these factors come first. According to the summary paragraph, the agency's approach "results in advertising that addresses clearly defined marketing objectives in a unique, memorable way."

The Disciplined Approach.   Many agencies operate with plans that outline the strategy. This is a way to impose some structure or discipline upon the decision-making process. While many agencies use such forms or documents, not all of them focus on this planning process as *the key* to their success in creating effective advertising. However, some agencies do feel that the approach they use, the process, is the mechanism by which great or successful advertising is generated.

For example, The Martin Agency of Richmond, Virginia, says: "We employ a specific, step-by-step disciplined process for the development of advertising which includes the gathering of data, background research, advertising research, and the development of a positioning statement. . . ." The statement concludes, "The discipline of the position statement helps ensure tight strategy and clearly defined direction. . . ."

Tracy-Locke of Dallas identifies six key elements to be considered in developing a creative strategy statement. They are: target audience, user benefits, reason why, brand character, focus of sale, and tone.

Noble & Associates, which will be discussed in more detail in the following section, also operates with a clearly defined process. The agency's advertising strategy development system is called "Noblelink" and it consists of six steps:

1. Define problem/opportunity and the objective
2. Identify the consumer and trade audiences
3. Examine the purchase dynamics
4. Dimension the purchase dynamics into consumer need, category standards, and product attributes
5. Develop the strategic/tactical solution
6. Develop the execution concept

The Integrated Approach.   Some agencies responded with statements that discussed several different elements and how they need to be related, linked, married, or bonded, to one another. For example, BBDO feels that the only way products can be differentiated by means other than performance claims is by "marrying the 'Product' (performance) image to a 'You' (user) image." The BBDO statement analyzes the limitations of product performance to explain how advertising must mix "Product" and "You" imagery.

The BBDO statement says, "The secret of great advertising is the *way* 'Product' and 'You' are married. They must be married seamlessly." The statement continues: "When an advertisement focuses primarily on 'Product' benefits to the exclusion of the 'You' dimension, it is likely to be a *cold* execution. Likewise, an advertisement focusing solely on the 'You' at the expense of the 'Product' tends to produce an empty execution." The BBDO philosophy concludes: "The head says, 'I get it.' The gut says, 'I like it.'"

Altschiller Reitzfeld believes that in order to create perceived differences that are dramatic and memorable, it is necessary to establish an "emotional bond between the product and the consumer." Altschiller Reitzfeld sees advertising as a dialogue between product and person. The statement explains, "This conversation between the consumer and the product creates a kind of 'emotional reason why,' a bond often more compelling than a 'tangible reason why.'"

Noble & Associates from Springfield, Missouri, specializes in food advertising, and the agency recognizes that the most effective food advertising says one thing and says it well. The key is to identify what that one thing is. Noble calls it the "Key Link." The process is to evaluate the purchase dynamics in terms of (a) the greatest consumer need, (b) the category standard by which all brands are judged, and (c) the actual product attributes. These are linked together to create the "Key Link."

Long, Haymes & Carr of Winston-Salem believes that great advertising is "Provocative Truth." The approach focuses on an important fact about the product and links that to a consumer need. The agency's statement describes its view of great advertising: "It is advertising that is strategically sound, based on some essential attribute or core truth about the product or service or company that offers the most promise to the consumer." The statement explains that it is advertising about a product attribute "that has been given a consumer relevant interpretation."

Other Approaches

The Organizational Approach.   A number of agencies said that great advertising was a product of great people. Lois, in his description of the LOIS/ GGK approach, writes: "To achieve great results requires extraordinary talent. We have that. Our creative department is comprised of senior writers and senior art directors. Many of the veteran creative people have worked with me for thirty years—and more!"

Other agencies pointed to the quality of their people but also described how the agency set up staffing and management. Beber Silverstein & Partners of Miami explains it this way: "Our people are chosen for their national reputations and their seasoned abilities to cut to the very heart of complex marketing situations. Most critical, however, is their talent for finding the approach that will persuade someone to act." Beber Silverstein also describes its group system, including its creative group heads and teams and how they work.

Tucker Wayne/Luckie & Company of Atlanta makes extensive use of creative teams and also describes how the creative teams approach the development of an advertisement.

AC & R/CCL of Irvine, California says effective advertising comes from a mix of things. "Outstanding advertising, we believe, is an alchemy of relationships: art and science, left brain and right brain, client and agency." The key, however, is the meeting where the pieces all come together. "The crucible in which much of the amalgamation takes place is a special meeting conducted at remote locations where creative teams work directly with clients to gather background information, discuss strategies and tactics and explore creative directions." AC & R/CCL believes that with its approach, "the best minds on the client and the agency sides are focused on the problems at hand with an intensity reminiscent of a burning glass. The experiment always succeeds. And, yes, the result is pure gold."

The Multifocused Approaches.   A number of agencies responded with statements that included many, if not all, of the dimensions of effective advertising discussed in the first section. Their answers were all-inclusive and, thus, couldn't be grouped easily with those statements that were more single-minded in approach.

Avrett, Free & Ginsberg, a New York agency, sees effective advertising as based on the three main areas of strategic analysis, ultimate buying research, and the agency's five critical elements of creative philosophy. Strategic analysis considers the competition, the best prospects, and the best buying appeals. Research translates product attributes into end benefits and describes what emotional, as well as practical, rewards the consumer receives. The five elements of Avrett, Free's creative philosophy include impact, persuasion, brand linkage, brand personality, and magic.

The statement by the Elkman Advertising Agency in Bala Cynwyd, Pennsylvania, focuses first on the creative work plan, second on the creative team, and third on the value the agency places on unusual, inventive concepts.

Tracy-Locke has a list of seven characteristics of good creative strategy. The seven elements include brevity; simplicity and clarity; competitiveness; the elimination of executional overtones; long-term appeal; one key idea; and a consideration of what the competition is saying.

Earle Palmer Brown, an agency in Bethesda, Maryland, has a three-part approach to effective advertising. "Our creative philosophy is simple. We believe in advertising that's direct, dramatic, and distinctive." According to EPB, direct advertising "has the right competitive strategy, gets to the point fast, and leaves the consumer with a clear, concise understanding of the major benefit." About drama the agency states: "Advertising that's dramatic gets the attention of the consumer and demands to be noticed." The third characteristic is distinctiveness. EPB explains, "Advertising that's distinctive has a look and feel that is true to the advertiser, and can provide a long-term 'brand personality.'"

Cole and Weber of Seattle responded with a list of thirteen dos and don'ts that outlines the agency's creative philosophy and provides direction for its creative people.

CONCLUSION

This section has discussed thirty-three agency statements and grouped them into twelve categories of approaches to effective advertising. There is a variety here, but there is also a foundation of basic concepts that runs throughout. Most are concerned with the product and how it can serve the prospects' needs. Advertising that is effective creates the message that best expresses this product–prospect relationship. In addition, the message has to be intrusive enough to battle through the clutter in the contemporary media marketplace.

The following section presents the agency responses. Most of the agencies sent samples of their work to illustrate their statements, and those are also included.

3
IN THEIR OWN WORDS

AC & R/CCL Advertising

(Irvine, California)

It's the little things that give life its special magic. Like romping in a big pile of autumn leaves. Dreaming of unicorns in a cozy room full of stuffed animals. Or putting an old Tennessee walking horse through its paces on a lazy afternoon.

Childhood's small pleasures. But for seven-year-old Kellie Ward, they are also some of life's small miracles.

Kellie is a cystic fibrosis patient. A disease which day by day robs her of her breath. But not of her dreams. And that's something her pediatrician, Dr. Garrett Adams, understands well.

About two years ago, Dr. Adams referred Kellie to Caremark Homecare. Working with him, Caremark provides the IV antibiotic therapy that helps her battle the persistent lung infections common to children with cystic fibrosis. Therapy that gives Kellie the freedom to dream. To ride. To make plans for tomorrow. You see, at Caremark Homecare we believe in magic, too.

Caremark Homecare. Because life should be worth living.℠

CAREMARK
Affiliate Baxter Healthcare Corporation

An example of the creative work of AC & R/CCL.

AC & R/CCL Advertising

(Irvine, California)

There is no such thing as an AC&R/CCL ad. There is no formula used to create advertising for our clients because we are committed to *not* repeating what has been done before. And, while the familiar is comfortable and big ideas are often uncomfortable, we try to provide as many truly unique options for our clients as possible. We feel that the role of the advertising agency is to provide a steady stream of creative ideas to the client, in sharp contrast to the single idea, take-it-or-leave-it mentality so prevalent in agencies today.

Outstanding advertising, we believe, is an alchemy of relationships: art and science, left brain and right brain, client and agency. The crucible in which much of the amalgamation takes place is a special meeting conducted at remote locations where creative teams work directly with clients to gather background information, discuss strategies and tactics and explore creative directions. Using techniques developed over the years, the best minds on the client and the agency sides are focused on the problems at hand with an intensity reminiscent of a burning glass. The experiment always succeeds. And, yes, the result is pure gold.

Al Paul Lefton Company Inc.

(New York, New York)

IRELAND
UNITED KINGDOM
NETHERLANDS
DENMARK
GERMANY
LUXEMBOURG

FROM BRUSSELS SPROUTS EUROPE

PORTUGAL
SPAIN
FRANCE
ITALY
GREECE

It's easy to see why Brussels is the heart and capital of the new Europe. And no one knows Brussels like Sabena.

Only Sabena's Common Market Express takes you there in 747 comfort and style. Call your travel agent or Sabena today. Because Brussels and Sabena are in a class all their own.

SABENA
BELGIAN WORLD AIRLINES
THE OFFICIAL AIRLINE OF THE COMMON MARKET CAPITAL.

An example of the creative work of Al Paul Lefton Company Inc.

Al Paul Lefton Company Inc.

(New York, New York)

Our approach to the creative product is rooted in a healthy respect for three terrible truths about advertising:

1. Our prospect isn't sitting on his hands waiting for our ad.
2. He won't work at it.
3. He has no interest in committing it to memory.

That's why we put enormous effort into the search for creative executions that are:

- arresting—to get our prospects' attention;
- clear—to be understood and;
- distinctive—to be sure our prospect remembers not only what was said, but also who said it!

Miss on any one of those counts and you've missed the boat.

Nowhere is this reality more treacherous than in situations where the competition markets similar products or services. The very fact that there is similarity in the competitive environment puts a premium on being distinctive. Being different.

It also puts a premium on translating the disciplines of arresting, focused and distinctive executions to every piece of communications we create—from television to four-color spreads, to small space newspaper, to collateral materials.

We have a credo here: *Together is the answer.* We say it. We believe it. Day after day, year after year, ad after ad. We listen to the client. We expect him to listen to us.

It works. And maybe it's one of the key reasons why we keep clients three times longer than the industry average. *Together is the answer.*

Altschiller Reitzfeld Inc.

(New York, New York)

If a video system isn't worth hearing, it isn't worth seeing.

by Ray Charles

"My word, have you ever seriously *listened* to most video systems? This is not great sound, my friend, this is noise. They may give you something pretty to look at, but they sure make you pay with your ears.

Then one day the Pioneer folks ask me to listen to their videodisc system called LaserDisc. And I'm amazed. The sound on LaserDisc is every bit as good as I ever heard on my stereo.

Maybe better.

I think to myself, 'If the sound is so great, maybe the picture isn't so hot.' So I ask the experts. And they tell me that the picture on LaserDisc is so much better than any other video system, nothing else even comes close.

And then they tell me that because the disc is read by a beam of light instead of a video head or a needle, it can't wear out the way tapes or records do.

Suddenly, it all becomes very clear to me: if you could get the best sound and the best picture from the same system, if you didn't have to give up one to get the other, how could you possibly consider anything else?

I don't care if you're a big video-music fan, or all you do is watch movies. Either way, you're not going to do better than LaserDisc nohow."

Model shown LD-700

⏻ PIONEER®
Video for those who really care about audio.

An example of the creative work of Altschiller Reitzfeld Inc.

Altschiller Reitzfeld Inc.

(New York, New York)

Given the number of competing brands in the marketplace, and the increasing difficulty of creating products and services with substantial product differences, we're convinced today's advertiser must be capable of creating perceived differences that are far more dramatic and memorable.

At Altschiller Reitzfeld, we achieve these perceptual differences by establishing what we call an *emotional* bond between the product and the consumer. By tone of voice, by language, by empathy, the consumer comes to believe that the product or service being offered "understands" his needs and because it understands them, offers a meaningful solution to those needs.

Advertising thus becomes a dialogue between product and person discussing their common experiences, the attitudes they share, their mutual understanding. This conversation between the consumer and the product creates a kind of "emotional reason why," a bond often more compelling than a "tangible reason why."

When there are real product differences, creating this emotional bond gives these differences relevance and makes them memorable. Where there are no substantive product differences, emotional bonding becomes a compelling reason in itself.

Asher/Gould Advertising

(Los Angeles, California)

Do your
soles need saving?

In order to save your feet from hell, call this number.

FOOT REFERRAL
For a qualified Podiatrist in your area call:
800·FOR·FEET

Arch Du Triumph?

If your feet hurt from wearing the latest French pumps, give us a call.

FOOT REFERRAL
For a qualified Podiatrist in your area call:
800·FOR·FEET

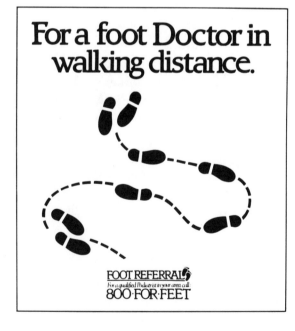

For a foot Doctor in
walking distance.

FOOT REFERRAL
For a qualified Podiatrist in your area call:
800·FOR·FEET

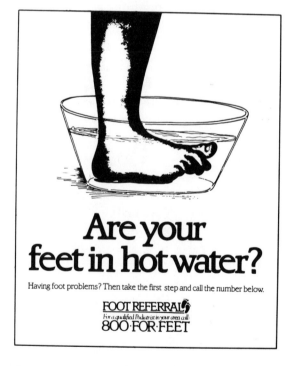

Are your
feet in hot water?

Having foot problems? Then take the first step and call the number below.

FOOT REFERRAL
For a qualified Podiatrist in your area call:
800·FOR·FEET

Examples of the creative work of Asher/Gould Advertising (copywriter, Ted Luciani; art director, Marcia Loots-Serna; account executive, Hal Asher).

Asher/Gould Advertising

(Los Angeles, California)

Our creative work is built on these principles:

1. What you say is as important as how you say it.

We are a content agency. Unless the strategy is correct, the creative work, no matter how clever, brilliant, funny, or touching, will fail. There is nothing so wasteful of time, energy, and money as advertising that says the wrong thing to the wrong people. We do not regard advertising as an art form. We are paid to move people to do things. To sell.

2. We believe in performance claims.

Although user-imagery plays an important part in our executional repertoire, our advertising is, for the most part, built on performance claims: "More videotapes," "tastier chicken," "bigger beer taste," etc.

3. We go for the clear, high-ground position.

We believe in copy that is simple, to the point, and easy to understand. We do not obfuscate. We accept the challenge of building our advertising around "the best possible claim," even if that claim has been usurped by a competitor. It is our job to find a different and better way to execute the "high-ground strategy."

4. Our advertising always has competitive urgency.

Our direct response and retail advertising experience has taught us to "ask for the order," even if all we're selling is a six-pack of beer. We try to excite people—to "push" them to react to our advertising by rushing to do something now.

Avrett, Free & Ginsberg, Inc.

(New York, New York)

UNISOM

"FLOATING"

COMM'L NO.: PFLP 3190

LENGTH: 30 SECONDS

ANNCR (VO): You're up...you can't sleep. Are you going to take just any sleep aid

or is tonight the night you join the millions who've switched to Unisom?

(SFX: BURSTING PILL)

Unisom is unique...only Unisom contains Doxylamine.

(SFX: TICKING PILL)
In medical tests,

people fell asleep faster...an average of 23 minutes faster than without Unisom.

(SFX: TICKING PILL)
No wonder Unisom is...

(SFX: TICKING PILL)
America's No. 1 sleep aid. So join the millions who've switched to Unisom.

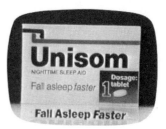

(SFX: TICKING PILL)
ANNCR: Take Unisom and fall asleep faster.

Avrett, Free & Ginsberg, Inc.

(New York, New York)

Avrett, Free & Ginsberg, Inc. sees effective advertising based on three main areas: strategic analysis, ultimate buying research, and five critical elements of creative philosophy.

I. STRATEGIC ANALYSIS

As the first step, we seek to answer the following questions:

- Who are we competing against?
- Who are our best prospects?
- What buying appeals have the greatest leverage?

II. ULTIMATE BUYING RESEARCH

This research . . .

- translates product attributes into end benefits, and
- describes not what marketing puts in, but what the consumer takes away with emotional as well as practical rewards.

III. FIVE CRITICAL ELEMENTS

Our creative philosophy includes five critical elements which we consistently strive to include.

1. Impact. Great emphasis is placed on impact, as the first (but not only) prerequisite of advertising effectiveness.
2. Persuasion. We seek to include the strongest consumer end-benefit as key to persuasion.
3. Brand Linkage. We seek strong visual and verbal devices which firmly marry a message to a brand image.
4. Brand Personality. We seek to create a total personality for a brand which goes beyond brand messages to an overall product image.
5. Magic. We believe in visual as well as verbal impact.

We also believe in an objective evaluation of copy effectiveness, including memorability and persuasion measures.

BBDO

(New York, New York)

An example of the creative work of BBDO.

BBDO

(New York, New York)

IMAGERY THAT WORKS

Increasingly, we live in an age of perceived parity in most product/service performance.

Products with "performance" edges are quickly imitated, becoming very nearly indistinguishable. Today's latest technological advances (personal computers, VCR's, CD's and 35mm cameras, for instance) are tomorrow's shake-outs; today's entertainment innovation ("Miami Vice") is tomorrow's clone. We are seeing the "commoditization" of entire industries.

This *perceived parity* poses a dilemma central to the entire process of selling through the media: *How can products be differentiated by means other than performance claims alone?* BBDO believes this can only be accomplished by marrying the "Product" (Performance) image to a "You" (User) image in focused *selling messages.*

Why do we say this?

People do not experience products or their performance directly through advertising—that can come from sampling or past experience, but not from advertising.

From advertising, people experience *images* of the product and its performance, and *images* of the users—people the advertiser associates with the product. Often these images are mixed together.

The key thing we must remember is this: It's all images. Advertising is all vicarious experience for the viewer.

Why "Product" and "You"?

As critical as the "Product" image is in any advertising campaign, it carries certain limitations:

- Many product edges (advantages) are short lived, and can be quickly copied and/or blunted by the competition;
- Many product "edges," as perceived by the advertiser, are not really important to the consumer;
- Many product claims address expected category issues, but don't really address the underlying consumer problems;

50

- Often, these performance claims provide little added value;
- Finally, what is meant to be a differentiating claim can sometimes have the opposite effect on consumers—and lead to perceived parity, as when imagery and experience do not match.

Therefore, we say that the "You" image is critical, because:

- It takes positioning beyond logic, and into the realm of emotion;
- It adds value to the performance claims;
- It can build product relevance *and* product personality;
- It puts the product truths and benefits into a meaningful framework for the consumer.

The "You" image takes the consumer beyond fact, and into feeling. It can build brand loyalty and help provide competitive insulation.

In fact, the appropriate "You" image can make the consumer feel like a smart shopper, in the "right" company, better off, more attractive, appreciated, perceptive, savvy, etc.

All of these feelings are perceptions that then become associated with the product in the consumer's mind.

WHAT MAKES GREAT ADVERTISING?

All advertising campaigns mix "Product" and "You" imagery; the emphasis changes according to the category/brand situation, but the mix remains constant. The secret of great advertising is the *way* "Product" and "You" are married. They must be married seamlessly.

People do not divide advertising into "Strategy" and "Execution"—they perceive a single entity—the execution.

When an advertisement focuses primarily on "Product" benefits to the exclusion of the "You" dimension, it is likely to be a *cold* execution. Likewise, an advertisement focusing solely on the "You" at the expense of the "Product" tends to produce an empty execution.

BBDO believes that execution is strategic.

Creative artistry must marry the "Product" image and the "You" image simultaneously in the execution itself. Which, of course, is the way the consumer receives it.

The consumer gets a net impression from great advertising:

- The head says, "I get it."
- The gut says, "I like it."

Great advertising alters the landscape. It changes the target consumer's perceptions . . . it redefines the category dynamics . . . it breaks through media clutter.

Not only does great advertising sell (which above all it must)—you, the advertiser, feel proud to be a part of it.

BBDO STRATEGIC DEVELOPMENT

Every agency has a methodology by which it develops its advertising. You've just read BBDO's theory about what constitutes great advertising, and that theory has defined the way we create our work:

- Determine the best "Product" image
- Determine the best "You" image
- Ensure that the execution marries the two seamlessly and dramatically
- And, at all times, AVOID THE OBVIOUS . . .

We have a formal methodology for accomplishing these objectives, and have developed as well some proprietary research tools to provide special insights into the market and the target consumer. These are discussed in the next section.

BBDO PROPRIETARY RESEARCH

1. Understanding the Market

We think that it is essential to understand the market from the consumer's point of view. The consumer will frequently look at your product and see its competition in a completely different way than you do. Frequently, the manufacturer's competitive set is derived purely from statistical data classification, with no thought at all to the consumer who will buy it. So we think that it is important to define the competitive set from the consumer's vantage point, not solely from the manufacturer's vantage point.

Market Structure Audit.   To do this, we've developed a tool called Market Structure Audit whereby consumers, through sorting cards, will tell us which brands are alike. It's amazing how this research has led us to places we hadn't anticipated.

The chewing gum market is a good example. Wrigley had believed that chewing gums competed primarily on a sugared and sugarless basis—sugared competing against other sugared and sugarless against other sugarless. Our Market Structure Audit, however, discovered that the gums actually competed more on a flavor basis—cinnamons competing against cinnamons, mints vs. mints, bubble gums vs. bubble gums, etc.

"Big Red," for example, had never been considered a cinnamon gum, yet our study revealed Dentyne to be its major competitor. By comparing the two we found that we had a flavor claim against Dentyne; that it lasted longer, primarily because the piece is bigger. We developed a strategy that accounted for both "Product" and "You" imagery to communicate this fact, and in doing so made "Big Red" one of the fastest growing Wrigley brands.

2. Prospect

Once we have defined who our competition is, we focus on the prime prospect: *Who* currently consumes competing products? We feel that it's important to view prime prospects not just as demographic statistics, but as human beings—to consider how they live and what they do with their time.

Lifestyle Indicators (LSI).　Lifestyle Indicators is a tool we've developed which uses Simmons, or any other large data base, to relate the usage of your product to the usage of other products. Through this method we can determine whether your prime prospects drink wine or beer, if they travel outside the U.S., what kinds of cars they drive, what books they read, etc. Cumulatively, these individual characteristics give you a flesh and blood understanding of the prospect, as opposed to "Women 18–49, etc." Out of this you conjure a different kind of picture which is very helpful in strategic planning and creative development.

3. The Prime Prospect's Problem

We have found that the best way to get a purchase decision in your favor is to solve a problem for the prospect. There are two kinds of prospect's problems—"Product" image and "You" image problems.

Problem Detection System (PDS).　To help us understand "Product" problems, we've developed a tool called Problem Detection. This method approaches the product from a "problem" standpoint, as opposed to a "benefit-attribute" standpoint.

People are not necessarily creative, but they love to complain, and when they complain, they don't necessarily play back the obvious. What one gets from the benefit/attribute approach is, most often, what people have heard from advertising. That is, what they have been told. The Problem Detection approach frequently draws new insights, and drastically different conclusions than from a purely benefit/attribute approach. Test and retest situations, using both methods, have verified this.

A good example is dog food. When asked what they want for their dog, consumers most often respond with "nutrition" or "good taste," which is what dog food advertising has, by and large, stressed over the years. But when asked what problems they have had with dog foods, consumers complain about their dog's bad breath and the food's odor or mess. You can see from this example that this could lead strategically to some radically different planning. Plus, if you can pinpoint a problem that is frequent and pre-emptable, then you have some grist for the development of a not-so-obvious strategy.

Photo Sort.   To help us identify "You" image problems, we've developed a method called Photo Sort. We give typical consumers pictures of people, and ask, "Of these people, which use this brand?" What we end up with is an array of pictures of people who use your brand vs. others. An extreme example is canned beans—Del Monte users vs. Green Giant users. You would think that the users of these commodity products would be perceived to be more or less similar. Not true. One has strengths not held by the other. Again, grist for the development of a not-so-obvious strategy.

4. Position

Now we're almost ready to position the product, to write the strategy.

Brand Equity.   If we're still uncomfortable, we use Brand Equity trade-off analysis, which adds yet another leg to the research. ("Would you buy this, if you could pay less for that?" etc.) This helps to determine which are the most important "Product" imagery problems operative in your equation vs. your competition's and which are the most important "You" imagery problems to manipulate, focus on.

With this arsenal of information from the consumer, we are ready to develop the Strategy—The "Product" image and the "You" image—that will position the product.

Product Positioning.   The "Product" position is developed by both the client and agency in a true partnership. No one knows the product better than the client—and this knowledge, combined with BBDO research input (i.e., Market Structure Audit, Problem Detection Study), helps form the product position.

How do we use "Product" positioning to help break the parity perception, to differentiate our brands? Like all marketers, we isolate the key performance characteristics—however, we do this *not* by offering category *benefits*, but rather by solving consumer *problems*.

"You" Positioning.   To develop the *"You" position*, BBDO uses research tools such as Lifestyle Indicators and Photo Sort for insight into user dynamics and imagery.

But all agencies now explore beyond demographics. We all seek a deeper understanding of the consumer; we all seek the keys to *meaningful differentiation*.

This search has led many to a hypothesis: "America changes fast . . . Her values change fast."

This hypothesis has led to an equation: Values = Lifestyle; wherein many marketers/advertisers have come to believe that by depicting contemporary *lifestyles*, they are defining deeply held consumer *values*, as well as *differentiating* their selling message.

To this, BBDO says, "Nonsense." America may appear to change fast—but her intrinsic values change *very slowly*.

Has lifestyle advertising worked? Initially, yes . . . It was new. It was attractive, even aspirational.

But today, lifestyle advertising has become its own *Cliché Glut*. Agencies must move beyond lifestyle for meaningful differentiation.

Are these statements really different?

- 1960's: "My parents can't run my life."
- 1970's: "My wife doesn't understand me."
- 1980's: "No one's going to decide for me."

Not really. They are all statements of the same age-old, deeply held American value—*Independence*.

What changes then? The *expressions* of these values. The *attitudes*. These *do* change with the times.

Here are some expressions of today's prevailing attitudes:

- Aspiration: "I want to do better."
- Fun: "I want to enjoy my life."
- Hot: "I want what's in."
- Contemporary: "I want to express myself in my own way."
- Quality: "I want the best of what I can afford."

The overriding attitude today: THE NEED FOR CONTROL.

"The single dominant theme of our time is this search for greater control over your own life."

D. Yankelovich

What are attitudes? They are essentially *mental stances*—not lifestyle shots in a TV commercial.

Understanding attitudes can provide deeper insights into the consumer. It can lead to true differentiation.

Break the Cliché Glut.   "Product" Stance + "You" Attitude → Advertising
Examples of this follow:

1. Pepsi Cola
   The "Product" stance is Leadership. The "You" attitude is Contemporary ("Hot," "In"). The resultant combination is executed in the campaign, "Pepsi. The Choice of a New Generation," with award-winning commercials that helped Pepsi grow, share and overtake Coke in the supermarkets.
2. Gillette—Dry Idea Antiperspirant
   The "Product" stance is that it "goes on dry, stays dry." But this did not differentiate this superior performing product until the "You" attitude was added: Control, Aspiration. The resulting themeline, "Never Let Them See You Sweat," and the campaign featuring rising young entertainers, has helped revitalize the brand.
3. General Electric
   The "Product" stance is "contemporary products of good quality." The "You" attitude is Contemporary ("Hot," "In") and Quality ("The best I can afford").

The campaign uniting these elements is, "We Bring Good Things To Life," which has revitalized the entire company, and which has evolved over time to show General Electric as a leader in innovative consumer technologies.

And there are many more.

SUMMARY

If BBDO had to sum up its strategic approach—what differentiates *our* approach—it would be our belief that . . .

Understanding "You" in terms of *Attitudes* versus *Lifestyles* is the key to the differentiation of selling messages.

The key to BBDO's IMAGERY THAT WORKS . . .
The substance behind the work that gained us the honor of being *Advertising Age's* 1985 AGENCY OF THE YEAR.

Beber Silverstein & Partners Advertising, Inc.

(Miami, Florida)

This advertisement from Beber Silverstein sells the product not as a key to becoming a sex object, but rather positions a woman's wearing Sophia as a statement that she is independent, self-assured, true to her own values, and still feminine—like the perfume's namesake.

Beber Silverstein & Partners Advertising, Inc.

(Miami, Florida)

Our Creative Department is organized on the group system, with two Creative Group Heads. Each group consists of two or three teams (with at least one art director and one copywriter). Our Creative Group Heads are people who would otherwise be senior creative directors at $1 billion agencies or name-on-the-door partners. They're with us because they've found that our agency offers more growth and greater rewards.

Our people are chosen for their national reputations and their seasoned abilities to cut to the very heart of complex marketing situations. Most critical, however, is their talent for finding the approach that will persuade someone to act.

We're proud of the fact that our creative department has won more awards than any other agency in Florida. But our creative people do not make ads designed only to win awards, as many creative boutiques tend to do. And they don't develop ads designed only to "test well" on standard creative tests as creative people in not-very-creative agencies tend to do. They create ads that are designed to work in the marketplace where our clients must survive and succeed.

Our procedure for determining creative objectives, and the strategies to meet them, involve a four-step approach.

1. The assigned creative team or teams receive an intensive education, including:
   * an overview of the marketplace and the competitive environment;
   * specific marketing/advertising objectives, so our creative strategy will further the total business strategy;
   * briefings with client senior management and key staff members;
   * a review of diagnostic research, both qualitative and quantitative;
   * a study of information from secondary sources (newspapers, business magazines, trade publications, etc.).
2. For each creative strategy, we outline the message (benefit and reason why), the target audience, target competitors, and the rationale for the strategy. If you agree with that strategic approach, it becomes both input for the creative team(s), and the basis for evaluating different executions.
3. We develop several executions consistent with the strategy, and analyze each one until we agree on a direction to recommend to the client.

4. We evaluate all creative work internally through:
   - the agency's Creative Review Board, chaired by our President, Joyce Beber, who must approve every creative strategy, concept, and significantly different execution before it is released for client approval.
   - The Strategy Review Board, made up of all department heads. Its purpose is to evaluate long-term strategic planning. The Board considers changing factors in the marketplace, target-prospect trends, and other variables that point up new marketing opportunities.

Campbell-Mithun-Esty

(Minneapolis, Minnesota)

CLIENT: THE TORO COMPANY
PRODUCT: Snowthrowers
CODE NO./TITLE: XTNS8602 "Driveway/Power Shift"
JOB NO.: TOSNOM7008 **DATE:** June, 1987 **LENGTH:** :25/:05

CAMPBELL-MITHUN ADVERTISING
222 SOUTH NINTH STREET
MINNEAPOLIS · MINNESOTA 55402
612·347·1000

1. (MUSIC AND SFX UP AND UNDER)

2. Until now,...

3. ...plowing through...

4. ...what the snowplow...

5. ...left behind... (SFX: BOINK!)

6. ...was one of winter's toughest challenges.

7. Now Toro introduces the exclusive Power Shift snowthrower.

8. (MAN SHIFTS LEVER) The Power Shift...

9. ...automatically puts more weight on the front...

10. ...for a more powerful bite...

11. ...on winter's toughest snow. The new Toro Power Shift.

12. The only challenge left...

13. ...getting out of the driveway...

14. ...to go buy one.

15. (DEALER TAG)

An example of the creative work of Campbell-Mithun-Esty.

Campbell-Mithun-Esty

(Minneapolis, Minnesota)

The creative philosophy at Campbell-Mithun-Esty is:
  1. We believe that effective advertising consists of four elements:

* a pertinent, meaningful benefit (exclusive or unique if possible);
* stated strongly to the exclusion of all minor or extraneous promises or elements;
* in a manner that creates a singular, memorable and acceptable personality for the service or product;
* repeated continuously, consistently without deviation until the message or campaign is irrefutably proved to require alteration.

2. We further believe that there is no style, method or type of personality that is universally appropriate. We believe that every advertising method or technique is possible for almost every type of product and that attempting to limit the advertising to certain methods (i.e., "slice of life" or "humorous vignettes") tends to shortchange clients by precluding the possibility that "around the corner lurks a better campaign."

3. We also have concluded that advertising is a serious business (not just another art form). Therefore, "intuition" and "creative judgment" cannot be the major criteria by which conclusions are reached. We believe in the process of research to corroborate, validate, or even contradict judgment.

4. Finally, we believe that advertising must reflect a sense of reality and sympathy with customers' needs, desires, hopes, and fears. We must come into our customers' homes and lives as understanding friends and remain as welcome guests because of the honesty and good grace with which we present ourselves.

CREATIVE BLUEPRINT

Before writers and artists are asked to create the advertising, the following Creative Blueprint must be filled out and agreed to by the senior creative people, the account people, top management members at the agency, and the client.

The Blueprint consists of seven questions, the answers to which set the guidelines for the message and character of the advertising.

1. Business Goals

These will be the key sales and marketing goals which can be affected by positioning and advertising. They probably will be repeated from the long-range marketing strategy.

2. Consumer Profile

Whom must we influence? Think of a specific kind of person defined in terms of psychological as well as demographic characteristics, i.e., habit patterns, hopes, fears, attitudes, age, occupation, ownership of something, physical characteristics, etc. Almost invariably this will describe the kind of person to be considered in positioning.

3. Current Attitudes

On what attitudes can we capitalize? What must we overcome? Or are we simply unknown?

4. Desired Attitudes

What attitudes must we establish or change? What habits do we want formed? Do we want that person to know something new has happened, or become aware of additional product uses, or sample our product, or change a negative attitude or misconception?

5. Desired Action

Do we want the prospect to send in the coupon, or cut out a coupon and go to the store, or send in for more information, or look for us in the grocer's freezer case, or try the recipe, or welcome the salesman when he/she calls, or store away the information and decide in our favor when the buying decision occurs six months from now? (*This answer should be given in specific measurable terms, if possible, because the changes here should serve as the basis for measuring the effectiveness of the advertising.*)

6. Main Selling Proposition

What is the key message or selling argument that works with this person? Almost invariably, this will include the "certain kind of product" specification for positioning. It should be written not as copy, but as an expression of the idea in your own words. The basis for this argument will come out of your knowledge of the kind of person you are trying to sell and of your product.

7. Personality

This should be appropriate to the person and the key thought we are trying to establish. Usually it should reflect a unique personality in its field, i.e., modern or traditional, fun or businesslike, innovative or conservative, successful, friendly, etc. Sometimes this point can only be settled when a creative execution is selected.

Carmichael Lynch, Inc.

(Minneapolis, Minnesota)

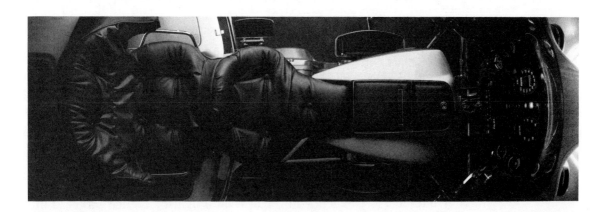

This Harley-Davidson magazine campaign is an example of an innovative use of the medium. Three half-page spreads were run on successive pages. The product was not new. The message was not new. However, the execution (by Carmichael Lynch) made this a breakthrough campaign.

Carmichael Lynch, Inc.

(Minneapolis, Minnesota)

Our mission is to be a creative company . . . in everything we do. For to create is to produce. To be creative is to be productive . . . yielding results, benefits and profits for our clients and ourselves. We can never be creative without being productive. By our definition, they are synonymous. The final measure of our productivity will determine how creative we are.

Externally: We must cause productivity through fact-based strategic planning, disciplined marketing planning, insightful consumer, product and communication research, impactful and persuasive visualizations and astute media placements.

Internally: We must cause productivity by sharing with all C-L employees our mission and also share the rewards of our collective goal attainment and to especially recognize and reward those individuals who made outstanding contributions.

Our only business is that of a full service, independent advertising agency "causing productivity" for companies located in our geographic region.

We strive to be an agency of balance, depth, and discipline.

Agency Balance: An agency influenced both by profits and quality of life. An agency equally influenced by marketing services and creative services working together in a healthy tension, neither force dominating the other. We seek to achieve maximum productivity thru healthy tension created by differing points of view.

Personnel Depth: We are dedicated to offering our clients the "best" leadership and direction in each of the full service agency functions . . . Stars backed by a competent and growing support staff.

Marketing Communications Discipline: We will follow a proven methodology . . . a marketing process, taking into account the full marketing mix . . . product, pricing, distribution and promotion. We dedicate ourselves to knowing the marketing communication issues of our clients' businesses as well as they do, spending their money as if it were ours. We will avoid "hip shots" and stress the methodological sifting of alternative strategies and plans.

OUR PRODUCT: MARKETING, CREATIVE, MEDIA

Marketing: We are dedicated to a disciplined process in the strategic marketing planning and advertising planning parts of our business. Dedicated to having plans and creative executions reviewed by top management and dedicated to attracting account management personnel with high social intelligence, motivation and work ethics, intelligence, team effectiveness, attention to detail and leadership skills. Strong account management keeps and grows business.

Creative: To strive to create advertising which is clear and effective in both intent and technical production. Our standards call for informative, quick, engaging, intrusive, cost effective and ethical advertising. We reject the kind of tasteless, demeaning, silly or self-promotive advertising which is all too common in our industry.

Our goal is to beat our clients' competitors in the same category. We attempt to beat them with uniqueness, importance and quickness while being measured by our clients against pre-stated objectives.

Media: We recognize that in the complex world of media buying and planning that large account "battles" may be won or lost on the media battlefield. Therefore, we are committed to creative media professionalism backed by state of the art media technology. We are committed to the concept of organizing strong, sophisticated, independent agencies throughout North America into an "in-market" media buying co-op.

Our goal is to be able to (in reality as well as perception) enjoy the broadcast clout of the largest agencies in the country.

Chiat/Day Inc. Advertising

(Los Angeles, California)

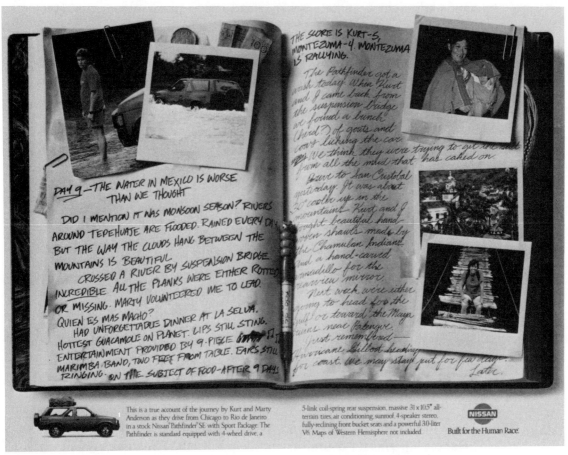

An example of the creative work of Chiat/Day Inc. Advertising.

Chiat/Day Inc. Advertising

(Los Angeles, California)

Our philosophy is centered on our end product: advertising that is

- conceptually and executionally instinctive,
- tightly focused on end-user needs, and
- relevant in tone and content to specific target audiences.

The real reason our advertising is effective is an amalgam of

1. an entrepreneurial clientele that is both reasonably permissive and demanding of both long and short term results, and
2. shared human values, a unique account team operating structure, and a loose–tight working environment.

ACCOUNT TEAM OPERATING STRUCTURE

Our accounts are staffed by tri-disciplinary teams; alongside the usual Account Supervisor/Executive and Creatives—on a day-to-day basis—we assign an Account Planner. The Planner's ongoing function is to continuously accumulate, originate, and synthesize data pertinent to the advertising's target audience; to independently pre-test, post-test, and continuously monitor—as an ongoing account assignment—both the advertising itself and the dynamics at work in its marketplace.

The result of this structure is a shifting and strengthening of individual responsibilities: the AS/AEs are responsible for the client–agency business relationship and for overall agency support; the Creatives are responsible for the conceptual and executional distinctiveness of the advertising itself; and the Planner is responsible for the advertising's target-audience relevance. In effect, we have integrated research, which falls under the Planner's purview, into our basic client service structure, as opposed to maintaining the traditional Research Department.

Our strengths are

- a winning attitude,
- a working environment conducive to the production of brilliant work, and
- an ability to thoroughly enjoy what we do for a living.

Cole & Weber

(Seattle, Washington)

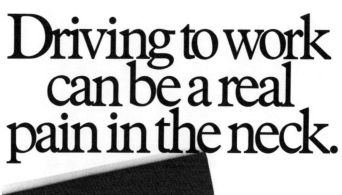

Driving to work can be a real pain in the neck.

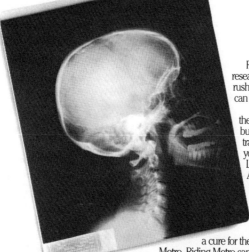

Recent medical research reveals that rush-hour commuting can take a toll.

Hunching over the steering wheel in bumper-to-bumper traffic can drive up your blood pressure. Lower your tolerance. And lead to all sorts of stress-related aches and pains— from headaches to backaches. Fortunately, there's a cure for these commuter ills. Metro. Riding Metro can save wear and tear on your car—and on you.

And you may be surprised how quick, comfortable and convenient it can be. As well as very economical.

If you've never tried Metro before, call 625-4500 and ask for our free guide, *How to Use Metro.* It tells you everything you need to know about Metro buses, vanpools and carpools.

Give us a call today. And find out about a painless way to get to work every day.

It's less stress.

This transit bus advertisement and the one on the following page appeal to the person looking for less stress in his or her life.

Cole & Weber

(Seattle, Washington)

Our creative philosophy is expressed as follows:

1. Never touch a typewriter or layout pad until you clearly understand to whom you are talking, what you are asking the reader or viewer to do, and why you're asking him or her to do it.
2. Be brave enough to try something new, quick enough to capitalize on successes and mature enough to accept your mistakes.

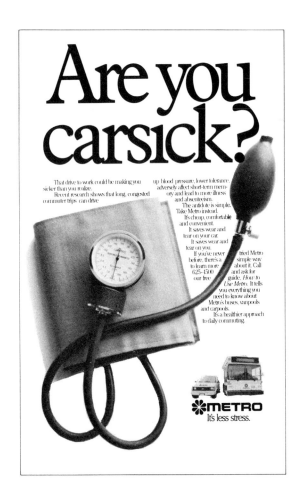

3. Do advertising that excels all other work in this field. This means being ahead rather than trying to keep up. It means creating new ideas in design, art, and copy.

4. Create advertising that has a personality.

5. Create with belief. If you don't believe, don't create.

6. Don't be a bore. You are creating an intrusion. And nothing is more aggravating than a boring intruder.

7. Use the English language in its simplest form. Fear clichés. Beware of superlatives, realizing they require a deft touch to be believable.

8. Be daring with words but never a daredevil. Be bold when boldness is called for, and write in a whisper when a soft expression can be heard better than a shout.

9. Write copy that speaks informally and directly—as though you were talking to the person you are attempting to reach.

10. Use the calculated understatement rather than puffery.

11. Be smart enough to realize the product you are advertising is not a panacea.

12. Write to a person's hands, feet, heart and mind. You want the reader or viewer to do something. To write for more information, to walk to a store that sells the product, to fall in love with your idea or to change an attitude. If your work doesn't motivate action, then you've wasted the client's money.

13. Be a simplifier rather than a complicator. Know what can be eliminated in pictures and copy without diluting the impact of the advertisement.

Della Femina, Travisano
& Partners, Inc.

(New York, New York)

"Bet the house on Liston. It's a sure thing."

Once again, what could never happen, happened. Once again, the underdog had defeated the favorite. And once again, people would learn—many the hard way—that there are very few sure things in life.

And the municipal bond business is certainly no exception to the rule. That's why there's FGIC Municipal Bond Insurance.

When it comes to the business of insuring municipal bonds, there isn't a company on earth that can do it better.

Why? Our unequaled strength.

You see, FGIC is now a publicly-held company, whose founding investors—owning over 80% of the stock—include six of the largest, most powerful and secure corporations in America.

And our capital base has increased five-fold through eight separate equity contributions. Today, that capital base is over 364 million dollars. And that's in cash, not in promises. And in this business, hard cash is the truest form of strength.

Few companies in this business have that kind of pure cash strength behind them. Or that kind of claims-paying ability.

Perhaps that's one reason why we can say with complete confidence, that we guarantee payment, in full, of principal and interest on every FGIC-insured bond—under every circumstance.

And why every FGIC bond is rated Aaa/AAA by Moody's and Standard and Poor's, respectively.

In short, FGIC Municipal Bond Insurance is one of life's few sure things—you can bet on it.

Further information is available from FGIC. Call 1-800-255-FGIC to learn more.

FGIC's founding investors include General Electric Credit Corporation, General Reinsurance Corporation, The Kemper Group, Merrill Lynch & Co. Inc., J. P. Morgan and Co. Incorporated and Shearson Lehman Brothers Inc.

FGIC℠
Bond insurance.
One of life's few sure things.

This advertisement, and those on the following pages, are examples of the creative work of Della Femina, Travisano & Partners, Inc.

Della Femina, Travisano & Partners, Inc.

(New York, New York)

The purpose of our agency is to create intelligent and tasteful advertising that reaches or surpasses our clients' goals and at the same time nurtures and rewards everyone in this organization.

Our philosophy is to realize that very few consumers lie awake at night thinking about advertising, and at best, they don't care about it. Realizing this, it is our objective to strike a bargain with them: We will interest or entertain them for a while so that they will listen to our message.

Obviously, this executional technique would come out of a well-researched position.

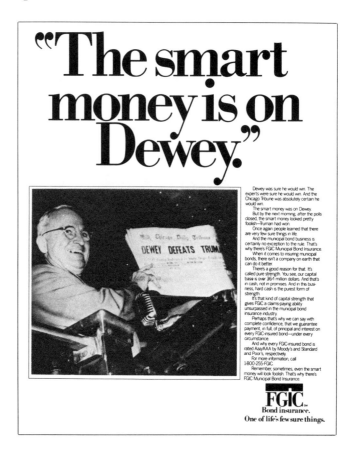

Earle Palmer Brown Advertising

(Bethesda, Maryland)

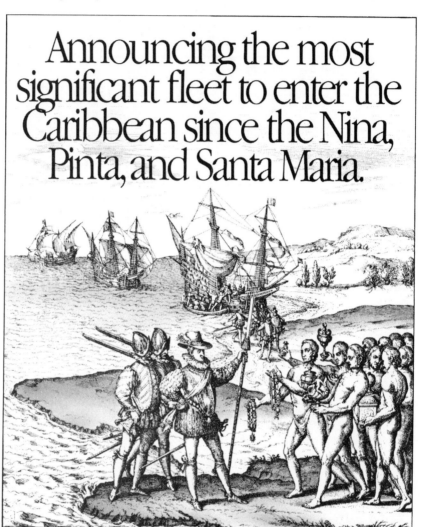

An example of the creative work of Earle Palmer Brown Advertising.

Earle Palmer Brown Advertising

(Bethesda, Maryland)

Our agency has become the most successful advertising agency in the Mid-Atlantic because of a dedication to innovative, competitive, creative work.

Our creative philosophy is simple. We believe in advertising that's direct, dramatic, and distinctive.

DIRECT ADVERTISING

Advertising that's direct is advertising that has the right competitive strategy, gets to the point fast, and leaves the consumer with a clear, concise understanding of the major benefit. At EPB, we pride ourselves on a dedication to developing a competitive strategy that's supported by research, relevant to the consumer's needs, and can occupy a unique position in the consumer's mind.

DRAMATIC ADVERTISING

Advertising that's dramatic gets the attention of the consumer and demands to be noticed. Since the first objective of any advertising is to get itself seen, this is a critical component. We excel at this because of our insistence on powerful graphics, strong copy, and high quality of production in our finished materials.

DISTINCTIVE ADVERTISING

Advertising that's distinctive has a look and feel that is true to the advertiser, and can provide a long term "brand personality." This means that the advertising "fits" the personality and perception of the advertiser. If one didn't know our client list, they'd be hard-pressed to go through a magazine and identify our advertising. That's because there's not an "Earle Palmer Brown look," but a look that's unique to each of our clients. Advertising should fit the client as comfortably as his personality, so the consumer can recognize the client and feel equally comfortable.

A. Eicoff & Company

(Chicago, Illinois)

Trade Support Television

(MUSIC: UP)
CHARLES WELCH (ON-CAMERA):
There's lots of ways folks like to eat our Pepperidge Farm breads.

I know one fella who's wild about all those plump raisins in Pepperidge Farm raisin bread. So he eats the raisins first, and then the bread. (CHUCKLE) Ooh!

And the minister's wife,

she can never decide between Pepperidge Farm caraway rye or classic pumpernickel, so she makes a sandwich

out of one slice of each.

And Bob's boy? He can put <u>more</u> food 'tween two slices of Pepperidge Farm oatmeal bread...and then...tch, tch, tch, tch...he delicately trims off the crusts.

ANNOUNCER (VO): No matter how folks like to eat their bread...they love the delicious breads and rolls from Pepperidge Farm. And, you'll find them, fresh, right on your grocer's shelf.

CHARLES WELCH (ON-CAMERA): As for me, I can't resist unwrapping these Golden Twist dinner rolls.

ANNOUNCER (VO): Look for the Pepperidge Farm <u>fresh</u> bread rack at these fine stores.

An example of the creative work of A. Eicoff & Company.

A. Eicoff & Company

(Chicago, Illinois)

Most creative departments at other agencies are judged by the quality of their work. Our task is to not only produce quality work, but produce quality work that gets results. Our concern, then, is strengthening our client's image and also making the cash register ring.

These are our objectives no matter what type of commercial we work on. We don't stop at award-winning commercials. All of our commercials' results are measurable; clients learn quickly how many products were sold or how many leads were generated. Since our work is accountable in this way, we must create commercials that viewers respond to.

At the same time, we must keep in mind the image of our client. Over the years, we've developed techniques to satisfy this concern as well. Our clients can't afford to air a commercial that projects the wrong attitude or gives them the wrong image. Though our focus might be results-producing advertising, that doesn't mean we compromise quality.

Elkman Advertising

(Bala Cynwyd, Pennsylvania)

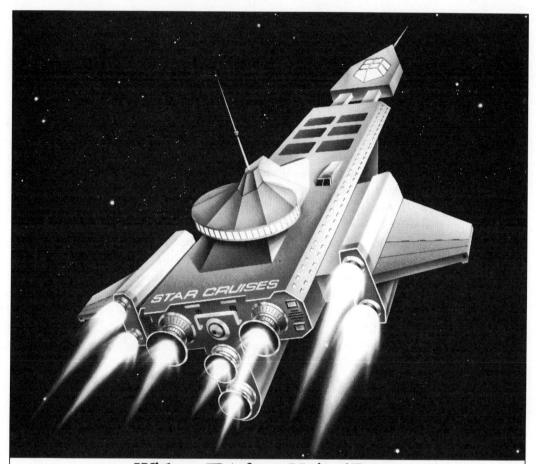

With an IRA from United Penn, you'll be able to afford that retirement cruise.

When you retire, will you be able to enjoy all the world has to offer?

You will if you plan ahead and invest wisely. And an IRA from United Penn is a great way to start. We have a variety of rewarding investment options to choose from, including fixed rate, multiple deposit variable rate, and self-directed IRAs. And you won't pay taxes on any of your earnings until you retire or begin making withdrawals.

Remember, the tax laws regarding IRAs have *not* changed for 1986, so if you make your 1986 contribution before April 15, 1987, you can still deduct the full amount!

Make sure your retirement is as exciting as you've always dreamed it would be. Come in and talk to the IRA experts at United Penn Bank. Explore the possibilities!

United Penn Bank
We work hard for your business.

Substantial penalty for early withdrawal before age 59½.

An example of the creative work of Elkman Advertising.

Elkman Advertising

(Bala Cynwyd, Pennsylvania)

Before we create any kind of advertising for a client, we formulate what we call a Creative Work Plan. This plan outlines all the pertinent information connected with the assignment—what the marketing objective is, who our audience is, what special problems may affect our creative executions, etc. With this information is attached a production budget and all the deadlines for approvals, revisions, and production.

Once the creative team has this information, the Art Director and the Copywriter get together to talk about possible approaches to the advertising assignment. At Elkman, we like to discover the unusual, fresh ways of looking at things. We like to use unexpected visuals, intriguing headlines, and strong concepts with pay-offs for our audience. We encourage our clients to take intelligent risks—to be willing to "stick their necks out a little" in order to get noticed. Because until you get noticed, it's hard to sell, no matter how wonderful what you're selling is.

Grey Advertising, Inc.

(New York, New York)

An example of the creative work of Grey Advertising, Inc.

Grey Advertising, Inc.

(New York, New York)

Our creative strategy begins with something beyond positioning. Beyond a communication of what the brand is and what it does.

It's the added dimension of *who* the brand is. A *who* which makes it recognizable and appealing to consumers. It's that extra dimension—*who* the brand is—combined with the positioning and the product itself that we call *Brand Character*™.

Product + Positioning + Personality = Brand Character™

A totality that expresses how a brand looks and feels to the consumer. What its unique character is that distinguishes it from its competition. That lifts it above the crowd.

The advertising that helps create that strong *Brand Character*™ has a look, a sound, a feeling as personal—as identifiable—as those characteristics which distinguish one person from another.

And, like the character of a person, it endures. The brand with a strong *Brand Character*™ is recognizable from campaign to campaign over the years.

In summary, we believe that a distinctive, appealing and enduring *Brand Character*™ is the major ingredient.

Griffin Bacal, Inc.

(New York, New York)

Radio TV Reports

41 East 42nd Street New York N.Y. 10017
(212) 599-5500

PRODUCT: G.I. JOE/HASBRO   87-11675
PROGRAM: TRANSFORMERS   5/12/87   30 SEC.
WPIX-TV   (NEW YORK)   7:51AM

1. (MUSIC) ANNCR: this is it, the Cobra Sea Raid.

2. MAN SINGS: Sea Raid... it's a fighting machine...

3. MEN SINGS: Out to blast Joe to smithereens.

4. ANNCR: Incredible Sea Raid splits to become a mini-submarine and a one man armored glider.

5. For attacking on snow and ice, the Cobra Wolf.

6. With twin laser canons and special ski torpedo.

7. BOY: It's the Teenovisor.

8. VOICE: Cobra Wolf is vicious on ice and snow.

9. Hot on the trail of G.I. Joe... (MUSIC)

10. MEN SINGS: G.I. Joe... the great American hero...

11. ANNCR: Live the adventure of G.I. Joe.

12. Cobra Sea Raid and Cobra Wolf, and other vehicles and figures sold separately. MEN SHOUT: G.I. Joe! (MUSIC OUT)

ALSO AVAILABLE IN COLOR VIDEO-TAPE CASSETTE

While Radio TV Reports, Inc. endeavors to assure the accuracy of material supplied by it, it cannot be responsible for mistakes or omissions.

Material supplied by Radio TV Reports, Inc. may be used for file and reference purposes only. It may not be reproduced, sold or publicly demonstrated or exhibited.

An example of the creative work of Griffin Bacal, Inc.

Griffin Bacal, Inc.

(New York, New York)

"We create advertising that works harder, sells better . . . and feels good!"

Joe Bacal
Executive Vice President
Director of Creative Services

Griffin Bacal holds a unique position in the advertising marketplace. We are recognized leaders in youth marketing. We produce more advertising directed toward children and their parents than any other agency in the country, and have an unmatched success record in marketing to young people.

Our audience of young people are among today's toughest customers. They are naive yet sophisticated, faddish and fickle, and brand aware before they can read! They are voracious for what is new. New looks, new sounds, new ideas.

To reach them, and motivate them, Griffin Bacal talks to them in their own language, on their own terms. Invariably, we take a new and distinctively non-traditional approach to creative work. We pursue the latest techniques in film and video, and develop the most contemporary music and jingles. Breaking rules, stretching guidelines and creating phenomena are the hallmarks of our approach to advertising. At all times, Griffin Bacal advertising thinks young!

G.I. Joe is a good example of our work. The toy figure was relaunched six years ago with a dynamic, kid-appealing "Real American Hero" positioning. The campaign catapulted G.I. Joe to the number one position in the toy industry where it remains today.

GSD&M

(Austin, Texas)

An example of the creative work of GSD&M.

GSD&M

(Austin, Texas)

At GSD&M, we believe that advertising is an uninvited guest in people's homes, in their cars, in some of the most private moments in their lives.

We must intrigue them—captivate them with the way we look, the things we say.

We must entertain them—encourage them to laugh, or at least smile; to cry, or at least feel empathy; and sometimes, simply to think.

We must persuade them—convince them that what we have to offer is genuinely unique and valuable to them.

Otherwise, it is unlikely we will be invited back. Successful advertising becomes an invited guest—the first step toward every smart advertiser's ultimate goal, brand loyalty.

Hill, Holliday, Connors, Cosmopulos, Inc., Advertising

(Boston, Massachusetts)

Real life, real answers. "Bill Heater" (Variable Life)
1986 National Advertising Campaign TV Commercial
To be seen in selected markets only.

John Hancock
Financial Services

VISUAL	AUDIO
Bill Heater Age . . . 30 Married, two children Income . . . \$35,000	I love you little Jenny Katherine. I've got something very, very important to tell you. Daddy got a raise! Are you listening? I got a raise!
Estimated Expenses Income Tax . . . . \$8,500 Rent . . . . .8,500 Food, clothing, insurance . . . . .11,500 Misc. .1,500 \$30,000	That means . . . umm . . . that I can buy you a sandbox, a playhouse. That means I can buy you a sliding board . . . a little bicycle . . . a diamond ring.
Needs Long-term security for his family To build investments	That means I can buy you a mink coat. Maybe we could buy a . . . or maybe we should put some of it away? Huh?

Answers
John Hancock Variable Life:
    Insurance with five
    investment options.
 	
    Stocks
    Aggressive Stocks
    Bonds
    Money Market
    Total Return
	What do you think about that?
	
	What do you know about the stock market?
	
	I love you little Jenny Katherine very, very much.

Real life, real answers. John Hancock Financial Services	Guess what? Daddy got a raise!

Produced by the Advertising Division for internal use only.

This and the advertisement on the following page are examples of the creative work of Hill, Holliday, Connors, Cosmopulos, Inc., Advertising.

Hill, Holliday, Connors, Cosmopulos, Inc., Advertising

(Boston, Massachusetts)

Four years ago, Hancock called.

We started to work and after a couple weeks we thought if we had to look at one more insurance ad we'd blow our brains out. The category was filled with ham-handed metaphor, bad analogy, a large fake rock and a cartoon.

And everyone was screaming financial services as if they'd just discovered the Rosetta stone for the future. There was a lot of noise, but not one was listening.

We had a prospective client with an agenda. He was in a hurry, and he wasn't fooling around.

So what to do?

A campaign emerged after many false starts and more than a few threats.

The idea became to tell the truth.

Which is never easy.

After a while we had an ear for what it should sound like (Heater), an eye for what it should look like (Pytka), but still something was missing.

Which is when the type on the black screen made its appearance (Easdon).

Now all the images were connected, the information linked. The work became whole.

Along the way a new client was repositioned. The consumer noticed. And happily, so did the world at Cannes.

Keller Crescent Company

(Evansville, Indiana)

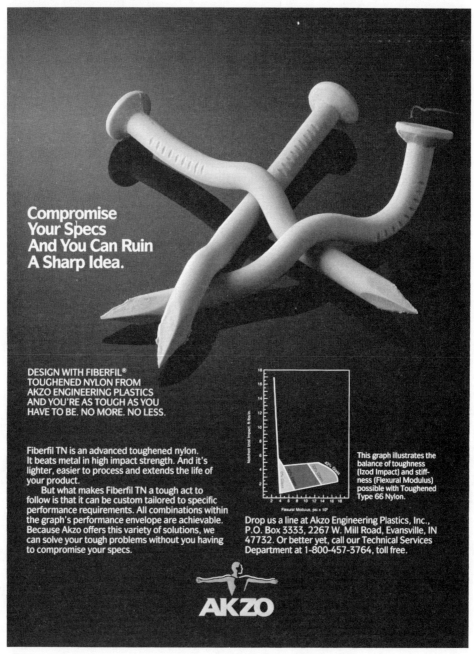

An example of the creative work of Keller Crescent Company.

Keller Crescent Company

(Evansville, Indiana)

Advertising's only role is an execution that solves your marketing problem. Therefore, we don't raise a pencil or a squeaky pen until we've isolated through client input, marketing, research and judgment the *one* major selling idea appropriate to a brand or an idea.

OUR CREATIVE BELIEFS

1. People are interested in products.
   People spend a major part of their daily lives using products and benefiting from products.

2. People are interested in advertising.
   If it is advertising that truly addresses itself to the interest they have in products. It must tell them something interesting about the product or enhance their appreciation of the product—just as though a good friend had told them about it.

3. Every product is unique.
   Every product, every service is intrinsically unique. And, there will always be a favorable difference that can be found in presenting it to the consumer.

4. The most important ingredient in any advertising is the "major selling idea."
   • real product superiority
   • market building
   • product personality
   • pre-emptive positioning
   • pre-emptive execution

5. Know the product in depth.
   Unless we know and have weighed all there is to know about the product and the market and the consumer, we cannot be sure that the major selling idea on which we are about to base our advertising is sound.

6. Know the social climate.
   What are the mores, the sensitivities—the environment in which the advertising is to run?

7. Use good taste.
   By that we mean, our customer's good taste. If we show respect for the type

of lives our consumers lead and the things they believe in their hearts, this respect is reciprocated. As advertisers, we will be welcomed in their homes.

8. Don't be avant-garde.
   Nothing is more fleeting than the veneer of today's trends. If you base your advertising on what seems to be current, you can count on your advertising being short-lived.

9. Don't use one style.
   We feel the product should show the way to the style. And indeed, being unique, should inspire a unique style of its own.

10. Be right, not expedient.
    We'd rather have a friendly fight on our hands today, than flop in the marketplace six months from now.

11. Be our own toughest critics.
    Sometimes that means killing our own brainchild. The more forthrightly and honestly we review our own work, the more likely it is to turn out better for our clients.

12. Earn the client's trust every day.
    We work best with our clients as partners—as extensions of themselves. Only to the degree that we display our integrity and tenacity for our client's success can we expect to be successful as an advertising agency.

Levine, Huntley, Schmidt and Beaver, Inc. Advertising

(New York, New York)

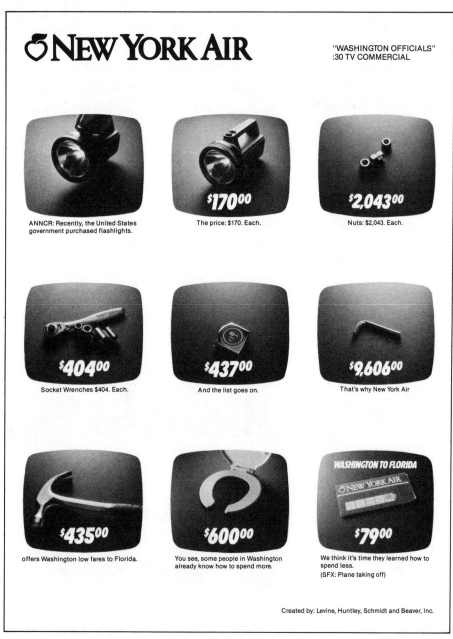

This advertisement and the advertisement on the following page are examples of the creative work of Levine, Huntley, Schmidt and Beaver, Inc. Advertising.

Levine, Huntley, Schmidt and Beaver, Inc. Advertising

(New York, New York)

We don't rely on rules, formulas, or gimmicks to create advertising. Breakthrough advertising can't be created that way. Nor do we believe in "creative magic." Great advertising is never just pulled out of a hat.

We create advertising simply by acquiring as much knowledge as we can—about the product, the marketplace, the competition, and, above all, the attitude of the consumer. We combine that knowledge with our experience and our instincts to develop a strategy and create executions that differentiate the product from everything else in its marketplace. To do this, we believe it is necessary to communicate with the consumer in terms that he or she can relate to. We therefore craft a personality for each client's communications program.

As important as the way in which we produce ads is the way we interact with our clients. We don't disappear for weeks and return with a creative product that we consider sacred. Instead, we seek our client's input and participation, engaging them in a continuous dialogue through every step of the advertising process.

Our approach results in advertising that addresses clearly defined marketing objectives in a unique, memorable way. Advertising that breaks through the clutter, touches people's minds and often moves them to action. That, in the end, is what we think advertising is all about.

LGFE Advertising Inc.

(New York, New York)

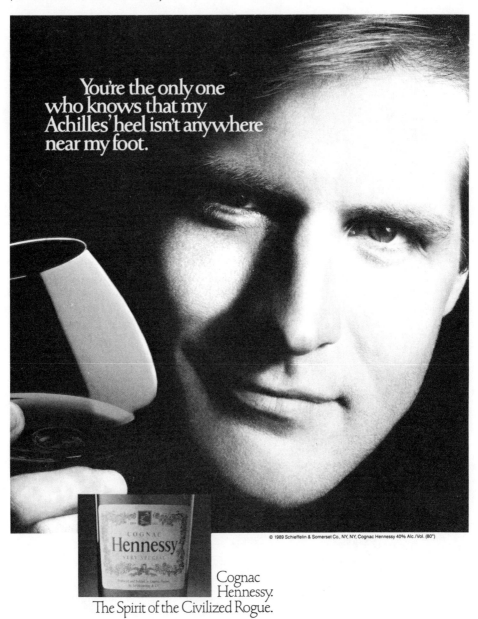

You're the only one who knows that my Achilles' heel isn't anywhere near my foot.

© 1989 Schieffelin & Somerset Co., NY, NY, Cognac Hennessy 40% Alc./Vol. (80°)

COGNAC
Hennessy
VERY SPECIAL

Cognac
Hennessy.
The Spirit of the Civilized Rogue.

A sample of the creative work of LGFE Advertising Inc.

LGFE Advertising Inc.

(New York, New York)

Good advertising, regardless of the product, service or company it presents, shares one central characteristic—it creates a connection on an emotional level between the consumer and the brand.

Beyond "intrusiveness," this kind of advertising comes as a welcomed guest into the consumer's home.

Only this kind of advertising can be expected to differentiate a brand, and motivate its purchase in today's competitive, increasingly commodity, world.

Liggett∗Stashower, Inc.

(Cleveland, Ohio)

In India, if some people were treated like animals, they'd be better off.

Notre Dame India Mission

The sacred cows are held in high esteem.
And the people have no self-esteem. Through your prayers and donations,
we can give the dignity every human being deserves. Please give.
13000 Auburn Road, Chardon, Ohio 44024

A poster created for a Cleveland charity by Liggett∗Stashower, Inc. for display in neighborhood schools, churches, libraries, and stores.

Liggett*Stashower, Inc.

(Cleveland, Ohio)

We work to identify the primary benefit of the product or its unique reason-for-being and then convey that benefit in the most interesting, informative or dramatic way possible.

LOIS/GGK

(New York, New York)

An example of the creative work of LOIS/GGK.

LOIS/GGK

(New York, New York)

My agency has a tenacious commitment to producing dramatic results through advertising. Indeed, we have a single-minded, almost fanatical commitment to the quality of the advertising we create. If our advertising is nothing less than great, nothing else matters—all the research, all the market analysis data, all the "full service" that so many agencies worship as the touchstone to great advertising.

We are doggedly committed to the belief that the work of an agency can and should produce miracles—if, indeed, only a miracle will do the trick. In the final analysis, what differentiates my agency from all other agencies is our absolute faith in the power of advertising. This belief, alas, is not uniformly held in the ad agency world.

To achieve great results requires extraordinary talent. We have that. Our creative department is comprised of senior writers and senior art directors. Many of these veteran creative people have worked with me for thirty years—and more!

We also believe that great advertising not only conveys what has to be said about a product—it also does it with a sense of theater and style that makes the creative product memorable and effective. Great advertising, we believe, in and of itself, is a benefit of the product! (We agree with Martin Mayer in *Madison Avenue, U.S.A.* that ". . . advertising, in addition to its purely informing function, adds a new value to the existing values of the product.")

Our creative modus operandi is to pair off the most suitable art director and writer on each account. This deployment allows us to distribute work among our key people so that each client is serviced by a superb team with a realistic workload. I oversee all of the agency's work and create many of our basic campaign themes. I also work as a hands-on art director on a day-to-day basis.

Here is the process we follow:

First, the agency's account team assembles all the background information and marketing intelligence available on the client's product or service and of its competitors. Additional research is implemented if needed. Client input is obtained. When all the information is assembled, a thorough situation analysis is developed. This summarizes all the relevant data, describes the creative problem as we see it, and outlines the objectives we plan to achieve with our creative execution. Essentially, we are "creative" problem solvers. This is evident not only in our final product—the kind of breakthrough advertising we do—but also in our clear, incisive marketing thinking, and in the timely, action-oriented research we conduct on behalf of our clients.

Our creative solution then has a transfer effect on *all* of the work we do as an agency—from TV and print ads to all collateral, sales promotion and direct mail activities. We are unashamedly "creative" problem solvers because we understand profoundly that agencies are first and foremost in business to create great advertising—and we understand fully that a great creative agency must be staffed by experienced, talented, hard working, marketing and media professionals as well.

As a natural extension of our graphic expertise, we are often called upon by our clients for design and packaging help—one more aspect of the great versatility of our unusual creative staff. Whatever the task—TV or radio commercial, magazine ad, newspaper ad, outdoor poster, in-house signage, direct mail flier—we bring to bear the same dedicated work ethic, a loving attention to detail, and extraordinary creative imagination.

George Lois
Chairman & Creative Director

Long, Haymes & Carr, Inc.

(Winston-Salem, North Carolina)

An example of the creative work of Long, Haymes & Carr, Inc.

Long, Haymes & Carr, Inc.

(Winston-Salem, North Carolina)

We believe great advertising is provocative truth. It is advertising that is strategically sound, based on some essential attribute or core truth about the product or service or company that offers the most promise to the consumer. It is advertising that has been given a consumer relevant interpretation in the creative execution that demands attention.

There are three questions we ask about every piece of work we do:

- Is it right? Is it true to the product or merely borrowed interest? Every product, every consumer/product relationship has an energy and an honesty to it that should drive the advertising.
- Is it powerful? Does it shock you, move you, enthuse you? Do you want to see it again? And again? Did it change you?
- Is it new? Is it fresh, pattern-breaking work or have you seen it before? Does it challenge the cliches and assumptions of the product category or reinforce them? Is it déjà vu creative or first view?

Provocative truth provokes action in the marketplace. It is advertising that has to be dealt with by the consumer. It is results driven. Attitudes change. Product moves off the shelf. The consumer buys.

The Martin Agency

(Richmond, Virginia)

An example of creative work of The Martin Agency.

The Martin Agency

(Richmond, Virginia)

We employ a specific, step by step process for the development of advertising which includes the gathering of data, background research, advertising research and the development of a positioning statement which creative uses as specific direction for their concepts.

The discipline of the position statement helps ensure tight strategy and clearly defined direction, and avoids problems caused by loose interpretation of these elements.

Noble & Associates

(Springfield, Missouri)

An example of the creative work of Noble & Associates.

Noble & Associates

(Springfield, Missouri)

As specialists in food advertising, we recognize that the most effective food advertising is that which says one thing and says it well. The key is in identifying what that one thing is. At Noble, we call it the "Key Link."

In food marketing, there is no single target audience. Rather, the advertising (and in particular, the advertising strategy) must be compatible with both the consumer and the trade; it must push the product through distribution onto the retailer's shelf, then pull it off into the consumer's shopping cart. The consumer and trade are inexorably linked together; consequently the advertising strategy, and ultimately the advertising for both consumer and trade, is developed in a parallel process.

Furthermore, as creative people:

- we encourage creative risk taking.
- we utilize every resource in the pursuit of creative excellence.
- we believe that "good enough" is never good enough.
- we believe outstanding advertising can only come through creative freedom, and that a singular, well-defined advertising strategy grants creative freedom.

Our advertising strategy development system is called "NobleLink" and it consists of the following six steps.

1. Define the problem/opportunity and the objective.
   This should come from the client's business/marketing plan, and paint a clear picture of the advertising/marketing environment, as well as the objective.
2. Identify the dual target audiences.
   Determine both the key consumer and the key trade prospects.
3. Examine the purchase dynamics (for both key consumer and key trade targets).
   Understand how the consumer uses and thinks about the product, category and brand and how the trade thinks about/uses the product in terms of profit, turns, packaging/pricing and the shelf environment.
4. Dimensioning.
   Evaluate (a) the greatest consumer need, (b) the category standard by which all brands are judged, and (c) the actual product attributes. These are ultimately linked together to create "Key Link." By linking together the ultimate

audience need, the standard or attribute by which all competing brands are judged by the audience, and the specific attributes or dimensions of the product/brand, the strongest positioning is determined.

5. Develop the strategic/tactical solution.

   Given the positioning developed, spell out the final advertising strategy.

6. Execution concepting.

   Develop specific advertising/communications concepts and executions, consistent with the strategy, position, purchase dynamics, audience and objective identified by the total "NobleLink" process.

TBWA

(New York, New York)

This advertisement and those on page 123 are examples of the creative work of TBWA.

TBWA

(New York, New York)

ADVERTISING BELIEFS

It is important not only that our people understand our advertising philosophy, but also that current and prospective clients understand it as well, because they then know what to expect from us and, in fact, whether they should hire us in the first place.

- We believe in proper positioning and the need for advertising to be sales-oriented . . . but we do not belabor these tenets because they are so obvious. Perhaps you have noticed, as we have, that the agencies which spend all their time pontificating about the "givens" (positioning and sales) tend to be the agencies which product the dullest advertising.

- We believe in the importance of the advertising execution itself . . . that how you say it is often as important as what you say.
  The most brilliant copy strategy in the world is worthless if the advertising is invisible. People remember ads, not strategies. Of course what you say must be sound to begin with, but those who think that the job is practically done once the strategy has been written are copping out.

- We believe that campaign continuity is vital.
  The average consumer is exposed to 1,500 advertising messages a day, so no matter how clever your advertising is it will never break through without consistency and persistence. That is why one of our principal up-front objectives is to develop campaigns which have "legs"—i.e., long-term staying power.

- We believe in the importance of production values.
  You can always get someone to do it cheaper, but lower price may not equate with better value. Naturally, we understand and respect budgetary constraints, but all things being equal we prefer to produce fewer ads and run each of them more often, rather than to compromise on quality.

- We believe that research does not inhibit creativity . . . unless you allow it to.
  It has become fashionable to make copy research the scapegoat for mediocre advertising. Nonsense. We use research extensively to help provide directional guidance. But we know that research is only a tool, so we always temper our final decisions with experience and judgment.

• We believe that one great campaign does not make an agency great; rather it is consistency of quality that is the true benchmark of excellence.
The best way for a client to judge an agency—and for an agency to judge itself—is to look across the board at the entire creative product. If the commitment to quality is as evident in a trade ad as it is in a television commercial, this means that the agency has pride in all its work, and that the quality of work produced on any given account will remain high regardless of which agency team is assigned to it.

Tracy-Locke

(Dallas, Texas)

WHEN IT CAME TO MAKING METALWOODS, BEN HOGAN WAS HIS OWN BEST INSPIRATION.

Introducing Series 56. The new line of metalwoods from the Ben Hogan Company, based on one of Mr. Hogan's most successful club designs ever, our classic 1956 woods.

Why did we adapt a traditional wood design to metalwoods?

Simple. We believe it makes a better club. Shaped by Ben Hogan's years of playing experience, the 1956 Hogan wood became a classic

because of its excellent playability. It was the natural model for these metalwoods.

Borrowing from the traditional design, Series 56 metalwoods set up visually square and allow you to align the ball better.

Yet, they feature the best metalwood technology of 1987, including

perimeter weighting for tremendous distance,

even with off-center hits. They're also the only metalwoods available with our exclusive Apex shafts.

And, as with all Hogan clubs

(including the original '56 woods), our metalwoods meet the tightest specifications in the industry for weighting, balance point, flex point, loft, and lie.

Uncompromising standards set by Ben Hogan himself.

Ask your pro about the new Hogan Series 56

line of metalwoods.

The only metalwoods we know of that've been 31 years in the making. And, we might add, are better clubs for it.

Hogan
PLAY THE BEST YOU CAN PLAY

This advertisement and the one on page 127 are examples of the creative work of Tracy-Locke.

Tracy-Locke

(Dallas, Texas)

We believe the characteristics of good creative strategy consist of:

- Brevity. It should be brief, reflecting a boiling down of numerous facts.
- Simplicity and Clarity. It should use simple language and be incapable of more than one interpretation.
- Competitiveness. It must identify why the consumer should buy the brand in preference to another.
- It should be void of executional overtones.
- It should be a long-term document not subject to frequent change.
- It should establish the one key idea which must be communicated for the message to be successful.
- It should reflect consideration of what the competition is saying.

Specifically, there are six key elements to be carefully considered in developing our creative strategy:

1. Target Audience
   The target audience is the person or persons at whom the advertising is aimed. This will normally be the person who makes the buying decision. Describe the individual you are trying to reach, not the mass.

2. User Benefits
   User benefits represent the advantages that will accrue to the user/purchaser upon use of the product. The physical characteristics of a product are not its user benefits. User benefits can come from research, but are often obvious. They are usually the reason why a person uses a product category or would prefer a particular brand. Be sure that each benefit is clear, simple and incapable of more than one interpretation.

3. Reason Why
   Describe the unique attribute or reason which makes possible or otherwise lends credibility or believability to the user benefits. Other products may claim the same or similar key user benefits. *You must have an important and unique reason why.*

4. Brand Character
   Brand character is the personality/image to be created for the product . . . the distinctive qualities that distinguish the brand. As such, it should help the

target audience differentiate the brand from competition over a period of years. Brand character differentiates a campaign from an ad.

5. Focus of Sale
   The four sections previously discussed collectively represent an inventory of all strategic considerations essential to the total advertising message. Now, carefully review these elements and select from them the principal basis upon which we are asking the consumers to purchase the brand: the focus of sale. It should reflect a firm decision to focus upon the one (or, at most two) key ideas upon which the sale stands or falls. The focus of sale represents the primary conceptual element to which the creative people will address their attention: the benefit promise they will seek first and foremost to render into a selling idea, visualize, and dramatize. As such, it is succinct, and very brief.

6. Tone
   This is the desired executional tone of voice for the finished advertising; its feel. This should describe as clearly as possible the emotional mood of the execution, and it should be expressed in specific understandable language. Brand character refers to the brand. Tone refers to the execution.

Tucker Wayne/Luckie & Company

(Atlanta, Georgia)

CSX Helps A Paper Mill In Tennessee Make Headlines Daily In Florida.

Bowater, Incorporated, is a major supplier of newsprint for *The Tampa Tribune,* a job demanding consistent delivery on a timely basis. To achieve this and hold down costs, Bowater relies on a distribution plan from CSX Transportation.

CSX moves the newsprint from Bowater's Calhoun, Tennessee, mill to Tampa in boxcars on regularly scheduled trains. There the paper is inventoried in a CSX distribution center until needed for just-in-time delivery by truck.

As a result, the *Tribune* enjoys the dependability and economy of rail transportation, better inventory control, and freedom from having to warehouse the newsprint themselves. Bowater benefits from greater customer satisfaction and the ability to supply customer needs from a nearby distribution center.

Helping papermakers and their customers meet deadlines is just one more example of the customized services we bring to all of our shippers' needs. No matter what business they're in.

We call it Partnershipping℠ For other examples of how we make Partnershipping work for paper producers and others, ask for our brochure "Success With CSX." Contact James A. Hagen, President, Distribution Services, CSX Transportation, 100 N. Charles Street, Baltimore, MD 21201. Phone **(301) 237-3458.**

Today's Way To Market.

CSX Corporation. Transportation / Energy / Technology / Properties

An example of the creative work of Tucker Wayne/Luckie & Company.

Tucker Wayne/Luckie & Company

(Atlanta, Georgia)

The creative process at our agency involves the extensive use of creative teams to serve all of our clients.

Each team (consisting of a writer and art director) is responsible for working within the discipline of marketing and the creative strategies which have been developed and agreed to by both the agency and the client before any creative execution can begin.

On major campaign development, multiple creative teams are put to work to generate maximum exploration of the agreed-upon creative strategy. This strategy will establish strong direction for the team, telling them who the target audience is, what the basic promise of the product or service should be, spell out the support for the basic promise and stipulate the kind of tone the advertising should have.

Unispond Inc.

(Oakbrook Terrace, Illinois)

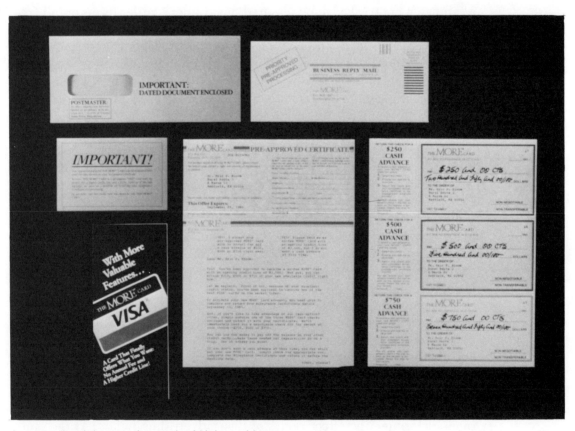

An example of the creative work of Unispond Inc.

Unispond Inc.

(Oakbrook Terrace, Illinois)

In direct response advertising, "greatness" is judged by results. Responses to a campaign are tracked and measured, via coupons, order forms or toll-free numbers, which show the marketer exactly how successful a campaign is in terms of cost per lead, cost per sale or bottom line dollars and cents.

Because of the empirical nature of this type of advertising, there are many influences to consider before the creative work begins. At Unispond, we first clearly define the target audience, then develop a sound marketing strategy and financial pro forma to determine the budget. The marketing plan then serves as a springboard for creative concepting. The ultimate goal is to create a one-on-one communication with each prospect. Utilizing information provided by our research and media departments, a highly targeted approach can be developed to meet the specific needs of the audience.

Direct mail is one form of targeted direct response advertising which provides writers and designers with an unlimited amount of sizes and formats to convey the desired message—from small self-mailers to three-dimensional kits. Copy tends to be longer in direct mail than in general advertising, because the objective is to give the prospect enough information to react immediately.

The designs and graphic techniques must present the selling proposition in a clear and easy-to-understand format. Creative techniques and involvement devices are often utilized to lead the prospect through the package and to increase the likelihood of response.

Although direct response advertising techniques are notably different than those of general advertising, the two disciplines seem to be merging. More general advertisers are employing direct response techniques to accurately determine the effectiveness of their advertising dollars. At the same time, direct marketers are upgrading the quality of their creative and production techniques to develop more aesthetically pleasing designs and to create a favorable long-lasting image.

Weightman, Inc. Advertising

(Philadelphia, Pennsylvania)

An example of the creative work of Weightman, Inc. Advertising.

Weightman, Inc. Advertising

(Philadelphia, Pennsylvania)

Our creative process is not a rigidly formal one, but it is also far from haphazard. We have a philosophy, a method of development, and a means for evaluating our work.

The philosophy is relatively simple. If it doesn't sell, it's not creative. The one true test of consumer advertising is at the point of purchase. We demand results by demanding advertising that is more memorable, believable and effective.

As we develop our work we look at what our clients' competitors are doing in order to spot trends and avoid clichés in the category. We use the products or the services. We want to know what the customer and potential customer sees and hears. We study all available research. If that is not sufficient, we ask for more. In short, we become the consumer in order to persuade the consumer.

We believe that for every product or service there is a Unique Selling Proposition, and we search until we find it. It may not be a real difference, but simply a preemptive presentation of a shared benefit. Having found the USP, we work very hard to present it in a way that is engaging, entertaining, believable, and persuasive. We avoid patterns. Just because one approach works for one product or service, it won't necessarily work for another. So we explore all techniques—music, humor, drama, etc. And after going through tonnage—quantity to find quality—the creative process gets us to one campaign.

We involve our clients in as much of this process as they want to be involved. And we have been told by several clients that they have never received such intense and continuing service as well as such a variety of ideas as they get from us.

That's how we do it. Now how do we evaluate it?

The Creative Department has its own multi-step review process, and it reports directly to the Chairman. The work, to be effective, must meet certain criteria:

- it must contain that USP that makes the product look or sound different, better, interesting;
- it must be clearly identified with the client, not mistaken for the competitor's; and

- it must be able to continue over several years and able to change to accommodate new needs or new competition.

We believe in personal judgement both at the agency and at the client, professional wisdom of people who know and work the business. And we believe in using appropriate research to confirm that judgement.

Over the years this process—this creative philosophy, method and evaluation—has netted us hundreds of creative awards. But we are not in business to win awards. We're here to sell. And the system has proved dramatically successful on that measure, too.

Young & Rubicam, Inc.

(New York, New York)

The creative objective at our agency is to be recognized as the creative leader in every market we serve and in every discipline. We consider correct creative strategy to be the bedrock of all successful campaigns and execution, no matter how inventive conceptually, will not surmount a weak or ill-defined creative strategy.

Execution (the manner in which a creative strategy is dramatized) is the flesh and blood of an effective campaign. We must have both. A sound strategy can survive a poor execution; brilliant execution cannot survive poor strategy.

Every Young & Rubicam account is subject to a long-standing, formal discipline which includes the following steps:

1. Examine all reasonable or promising strategic alternatives for a given product's marketing objective using a strategy selection outline document. Each strategic alternative is examined in three basic components of creative strategy:

   (a) product class definition (where the business is expected to come from);

   (b) target group selection;

   (c) message element.

   Each of these is supported by a rationale.

2. Having selected the best of the strategic options, we then apply the same process and analyze the product's competitive strategies to help sharpen ours and to avoid inadvertent duplication.

   Supporting this process are various informational documents such as brand personality statements and media work plans.

3. Once a strategy is selected, the strategy is recorded on a document called a Creative Work Plan, which becomes the consumer reference point for everyone involved in determining whether the subsequent execution is true to the strategy.

   The Creative Work Plan covers the key facts, consumer problem(s), consumer objective, principal competition, promised benefit and reason why.

4. Execution then proceeds when the creative strategy development process is completed. Properly drawn strategies do not dictate execution. In fact, they allow creative imagination to take flight. They insure that a proper course is maintained.

Mark Stroock
Young & Rubicam,
Inc.

References

[1] Lou Redmond, "On Writing Advertising," *Ogilvy and Mather Magazine.*

[2] William R. Swinyard and Charles H. Patti, "The Communications Hierarchy Framework for Evaluating Copytesting Techniques," *Journal of Advertising*, 8:3, 1979, pp. 29–36; Steuart Henderson Britt, "Are So-Called Successful Advertising Campaigns Really Successful?" *Journal of Advertising Research* 9 (June, 1969) pp. 3–9.

[3] David Ogilvy, "Ogilvy on Advertising," *Advertising Age*, August 1, 1983, pp. M4–M5, M48, M52.

[4] David Ogilvy, *Confessions of an Advertising Man* (New York: Dell Publishing, 1963); idem, *Ogilvy on Advertising* (New York: Vintage books, 1985).

[5] Sid Bernstein, "Ogilvy Spews Out Some Rules," *Advertising Age*, December 3, 1979, p. 20.

[6] John Caples, *How to Make Your Advertising Make Money* (Englewood Cliffs, NJ: Prentice-Hall, 1983); idem, *Tested Advertising Methods*, 4th ed. (Englewood Cliffs, NJ: Prentice-Hall, 1975).

[7] Carl Hixon, "Leo," *Advertising Age*, February 8, 1982, pp. 3–8.

[8] Fred Danzig, "One of the Most Ardent Players Relates Tales of the Ad Game," *Advertising Age*, September 5, 1977, p. 26.

[9] Leo Burnett, "Keep Listening to That Wee, Small Voice," in *Readings in Advertising and Promotion Strategy*, eds. Arnold M. Barban and C.H. Sandage (Homewood, IL: Richard D. Irwin, 1968) pp. 153–162.

[10] Martin Mayer, *Madison Avenue, U.S.A.* (New York: Pocket Books, 1959), pp. 56–58.

[11] Ibid., p. 58.

[12] Albert C. Book and C. Dennis Schick, *Fundamentals of Copy and Layout* (Lincolnwood, IL: NTC Business Books, 1984), pp. 3–4.

[13] Ibid., pp. 6–7.

[14] Mayer, *Madison Avenue, U.S.A.*, p. 68.

[15] Joseph Winski, "He Swims Against the Tide," *Advertising Age*, April 26, 1982, pp. M2–3, 6, 8.

[16] Tom Dillon, "The Triumph of Creativity Over Communication," *Journal of Advertising* 4:3 (Summer, 1975), pp. 15–18.

[17] Simon Broadbent, *Advertising Works 2*, (London: Holt-Rinehart and Winston, 1982), pp. viii–xi.

[18] Ibid..

[19] Ibid.

[20] Thomas E. Barry, "The Development of the Hierarchy of Effects: An Historical Perspective," in *Current Issues and Research in Advertising: 1987*, eds. James H. Leigh and Claude R. Martin, Jr., 10:1 and 2, pp. 251–295.

[21] Robert J. Lavidge and Gary A. Steiner, "A Model for Predictive Measurements of Advertising Effectiveness," in *Strategic Advertising Decisions*, eds. Ronald D. Michman and Donald W. Jugenheimer, (Columbus, OH: Grid, Inc., 1976), pp. 299–304.

[22] Herbert E. Krugman, "The Impact of Television Advertising: Learning Without Involvement." *Public Opinion Quarterly* 29:3, 1965, pp. 349–356.

[23] Swinyard and Patti, "The Communications Hierarchy Framework."

[24] Barry, "The Development of the Hierarchy of Effects," p. 266.

[25] Sandra E. Moriarty, "Beyond the Hierarchy of Effects: A Conceptual Framework," *Current Issues & Research in Advertising*, vol. 1, 1983, pp. 45–55.

[26] Kim Rotzoll, James E. Haefner, and Charles H. Sandage, *Advertising in Contemporary Society* (Dallas: South-Western Publishing, 1986), pp. 59–60.

[27]Ibid., p. 47.

[28]Kim Rotzoll, "What Factors Affect Response to Ads?" *Advertising Working Papers #5* (Urbana-Champaign: University of Illinois Department of Advertising, 1978).

[29]Ibid.

[30]Fred L. Schlinger, "The Measurement of Advertising Communication: Some Considerations," *Journal of Advertising*, 3:1, 1974, pp. 12–15.

[31]David Ogilvy, *Confessions of an Advertising Man*, p. 112.

[32]Peter Cornish, "Advertising that Gets Talked About," *Advertising Age*, November 16, 1987, p. 18.

[33]Ibid.

[34]S.Watson Dunn and Arnold M. Barban, *Advertising: Its Role in Modern Marketing*, 6th ed. (Chicago: The Dryden Press, 1986).

[35]Russell Colley, *Defining Advertising Goals for Measured Advertising Results* (New York: Association of National Advertisers, 1961).

[36]William H. Wells, "Transformation vs. Informational Advertising" (Paper given to Association for Consumer Research Annual Conference, 1981, St. Louis).

[37]Draper Daniels, "The Myths That Make It Hard To Create Advertising That Creates Customers," *Advertising Working Papers* (Urbana-Champaign: University of Illinois Department of Advertising, 1978).

[38]William D. Wells, "Three Useful Ideas," in *Advances in Consumer Research*, ed. Richard J. Lutz, vol. 13 (Provo, Utah: Association for Consumer Research, 1986), pp. 9–11.

[39]John O'Toole, "Keeping Our Part of the Deal," *Advertising Age*, March 1, 1982, pp. M33–35.

[40]William Bernbach, "Bill Bernbach Defines Four Disciplines of Advertising," *Advertising Age*, July 5, 1971, pp. 21–23.

[41]Danzig, "One of the Most Ardent Players Relates Tales of the Ad Game." p. 26.

[42]Wayne Walley, "Freberg's Back on Target with Non-advertising," *Advertising Age*, April 6, 1987, p. 60.

[43]Ibid., p. 60.

[44]Kim Rotzoll, "Gossage Revisited: Reflections of Advertising's Legendary Iconoclast," *Journal of Advertising* 9:4, pp. 6–14; and *Is There Any Hope for Advertising*, eds. Kim Rotzoll, Jarlath Graham, and Barrows Mussey (Urbana: University of Illinois Press, 1986).

[45]Ibid.

[46]"The Adman Who Plays with Paper Airplanes," *Business Week*, February 11, 1967, pp.74–80.

[47]Malcolm MacDougall, "Emerging From the Creative Coma," *Adweek*, November 30, 1981, p. 22.

[48]John Caples, "50 Things I Have Learned in 50 Years in Advertising," *Advertising Age*, September 22, 1975, pp. 47–48.

[49]Russ Johnston, "Marion Harper—Why His Mystique Lives On," *Advertising Age*, February 21, 1983, pp. M4–M5.

[50]Hixon, "Leo," pp. 3–8.

[51]Bart Cummings, "Charlie Brower Looks Back on a 45-Year Career," *Advertising Age*, July 25, 1983, pp. M34–36.

[52]Shirley Polykoff, "Will You or Won't You . . . Take a Chance," *Advertising Age*, February 1, 1982, pp. 45–46.

[53]Ibid., pp. 45–46.

[54]William Bernbach, "A Creative Credo for the Advertising Business," *Advertising Age*, April 30, 1980, p. 206.

[55]MacDougall, "Emerging From the Creative Coma," p. 22.

[56]Joseph M. Winski, "Kid from Brooklyn Grows Into a Power Hitter: The Book on Phil Dusenberry Is All Major League," *Advertising Age*, March 28, 1983, pp. M4–5, 29–30.

[57]Louis T. Hagopian, Speech to the Milwaukee Advertising Club, November 19, 1980.

[58]Winski, "He Swims Against the Tide," pp. M2–3, 6, 8.

[59]Ibid. pp. M2–3, 6, 8.

[60]O'Toole, "Keeping Our Part of the Deal," pp. M33–M35.

[61]Caples, "50 Things I Have Learned in 50 Years in Advertising," pp. 47–48.

[62]Gerry Scorse, "Ogilvy versus Bernbach," *Advertising Age*, Oct. 26, 1987, p. 18.